WHISPERS

among the

PRAIRIE

MICHELLE ROBERTS

First Published in Australia by Aurora House
www.aurorahouse.com.au

This edition published 2017
Copyright © Michelle Roberts 2017
Typesetting: Chameleon Print Design
Cover design, typesetting: Chameleon Print Design

ISBN number: 9780987617767 (paperback)

National Library of Australia Cataloguing in Publication entry:
Creator: Roberts, Michelle, author.
Title: Whispers Among the Prairie
ISBN: 9780987617767
Subjects: Historical fiction.
Dewey Number: A823.4

To the memory of Chief Black Kettle
of the Southern Cheyenne.
He fought hard on the peace path.

Contents

1

Morning Dove

Thump! Thump! Little Raven fell to the ground under the weight of his best friend Red Eagle. They loved playing their war games; they were still too young to be warriors. Dust was covering them both. Red Eagle puffed out, "You are weak, you are just like the White Man. You are not strong enough to be Cheyenne."

Suddenly, Little Raven wrapped his legs around Red Eagle's head and flipped him onto his back. "Who is not a Cheyenne now?" Little Raven said, laughing. "You are weak like the White Man and smell like him too." They both laughed.

A woman stood by her tepee, observing the day's activities. The children were busy frolicking in and out of the stream, swimming, playing war games and learning how to ride horses under the instruction of their elders. The tribesmen were mending bows and arrows, painting war shields and new tepees, as well as helping the young boys hunt small game. The women were preparing buffalo hides, sewing buckskin jackets, and collecting wild berries and onions for tonight's feast.

The woman by the tepee was lean and tall with dark mysterious eyes and raven hair that shone like black satin. Her delicate nose accentuated her angular face, and her senses were acute like a mule deer ready to flee from an enemy. Her name was Morning Dove, a Southern Cheyenne maiden. She was twenty years old — two years older than her brother, Black Beaver. Tragically, their mother and father died during a small pox epidemic brought to their village by infected traders years ago. The entire tribe cared for Morning Dove and her brother, and Chief Black Kettle became an enduring father figure to them. Morning Dove and Black Beaver treated him as such, and Black Kettle's wife, Medicine Woman Later, became the mother they needed.

Morning Dove was transfixed by her surroundings: an eagle soared above her gracefully; a coyote appeared close to the village, trying to scavenge whatever it could find. The summer would end soon, making way for the next change of season. The Southern Cheyenne would eventually leave the Smoky Hill River camp to prepare for winter. The afternoon sun was starting to hide behind the forthcoming clouds; a single ray stretched over Black Kettle's village, giving it a golden glow.

Morning Dove's attention soon turned to Little Raven and Red Eagle pursuing their war games, laughing.

Thump! Thump! Little Raven and Red Eagle tackled Morning Dove to the ground. "What are you doing? What are you doing?" Morning Dove cried in shock.

"We are playing war games and you are our prisoner," Little Raven replied.

"Go away you two. I am a woman. I don't play these silly war games. On you go!"

Little Raven and Red Eagle were startled by Morning Dove's assertiveness. They both started running around the village, making their distinctive war cries.

Morning Dove dusted herself off the best she could and made her way down to the river bed. She dipped her hands in the icy cold water and washed her face; she did this again and noticed an odd reflection in the water. It was the face of a Native American Indian. He looked at Morning Dove, transfixed. His long hair was worn in two tight braids accentuating his youthful face. This was all she could see. Startled, she looked behind her in case someone was there, but not a soul was around. She looked back at the water and the face started smiling at her. Feeling spooked, she ran back to the village, towards the safety of her tepee.

While Medicine Woman Later was walking through the village, trying to find Morning Dove or Black Beaver, she noticed Morning Dove running towards her. "Morning Dove. Morning Dove. George Bent is here for your English lesson and I don't know where Black Beaver is. He knew that George was coming today, he must be out hunting. I haven't seen him all day," said Medicine Woman Later.

Morning Dove stopped in front of Medicine Woman Later. She considered telling her about the vision but decided against it. "Yes, Mama. I will go and meet George at our tepee, I was just going that way. I haven't seen Black Beaver either, and I'm not wasting time looking for him."

"Are you alright, Morning Dove? You look a bit scared, as though something is worrying you."

"I'm fine. I better go and meet George now." Morning Dove hurried away. She didn't want to look into her mother's eyes, as she would see there was something wrong. *What did that vision mean?* Was trouble coming to her? She pushed aside her worries before walking into the tepee for her English lesson.

"Hi, Morning Dove," George said happily while sitting cross-legged in the tepee, waiting patiently for his students. "I have some new reading material for you today. Where is Black Beaver? Is he ready for his lesson?"

Morning Dove settled on the ground in front of George. "I'm not sure where my brother has gone. He may be out hunting with the other warriors, so I think it's just me for the lesson today." George Bent was William's son — a good and trusted white friend of Black Kettle's, who'd married into the Cheyenne tribe. Therefore, George knew both the White and Cheyenne worlds. He was educated at Saint Louis. As a favour to the great chief, George helped Morning Dove and Black Beaver learn the White Man's words, as Black Kettle insisted they needed to know them.

"Alright then, Morning Dove, we'd better start. Today we are going to read some extracts from this book and try to understand the meanings," informed George, holding up a book.

"That sounds hard. I know you have been teaching me for a few years, but the language is difficult to grasp and at times it doesn't make sense," Morning Dove said, concerned.

"Well, that is understandable, but you have learnt so much and come such a long way. Don't give up now, the English language will come in handy. Black Kettle wants you to learn. Your father is a great visionary of the Southern Cheyenne, and he knows this will help you. You have heard all of his stories about visiting the president in Washington, and he knows the White Man is one of many who will keep coming."

"Yes, my father knows a lot. He must speak to the Great Spirit, as he is very in tune with the earth and the happenings. I admire him so much and am grateful he adopted my brother and me. He has taught us a lot and he wants us to know the Whites' language because he knows we will need it, especially now that they are pouring into our country."

"Yes, that's right, Morning Dove. You cannot stop them, and it will benefit you to know the language so you can communicate with them when needed. But enough of that, let's start our lesson. You can read the first two sentences out loud and then translate them. You can do this, Morning Dove. You know a lot of English now."

"Alright, here goes, but you will help me if I get it wrong, won't you?"

"Yes, come on, just start," said George, trying to encourage her. The lesson continued into the late afternoon.

The children began trickling back to see their parents and it was time to bring in the large horse herd from the open prairies to their night time sanctuary. Women were organising dinner: collecting firewood, fresh water and preparing fresh elk meat to stew in pots, as well as buffalo ribs. A special feast was being held for coming visitors. There was excitement in the camp — there would be lots of dancing, singing and storytelling tonight.

"Thank you, George, for the lesson. Are you staying for the feast?" Morning Dove asked while walking out of the tepee with George, who was holding his books.

"Well, in fact, I am. Your father invited me. It will be good to see the dog soldiers again. They are fine specimens — so strong and bold."

"Yes, they are the pride of our village, they are very fierce. I know my brother wants to join them. I hope he doesn't as they make war all the time. I don't want to lose him."

"I am going to see your father now. I just saw him go to the far end of the village."

"I will walk with you," said Morning Dove.

As they were walking, Black Beaver appeared with two dead rabbits on one shoulder and a wild turkey hanging on the other.

"Black Beaver, you missed your lesson. What is your excuse?" Morning Dove demanded.

"My sister, can't you see I have been hunting? There is a feast tonight to honour the dog soldiers." He turned his gaze to George. "Sorry, George, but I just wanted to go hunting today. I will be at your lesson next time. I don't like the White Man's way of speaking anyhow."

"That is not the point, my brother. Our father wishes us to learn and know as much as we can."

"It is not going to matter if I miss this one time."

"Black Beaver, please make sure you're here for your next lesson. We are just going to find your father," George said.

Black Beaver nodded. "I am going back to the lodge. I will leave these with you, Morning Dove," he handed her the dead carcasses, "so you can skin them." Morning Dove stared in astonishment at the thought of performing such a ghastly task. "You know it is a woman's job," said Black Beaver, laughing as he walked away, knowing his sister hated such a task.

Morning Dove held the carcasses, not sure what to do with them, as she continued walking with George towards the end of the village where Black Kettle was meant to be.

Suddenly, Morning Dove noticed Red Eagle and Little Raven bolting towards her. Just in time she saw Black Kettle playing with some of the children, tickling them as they circled around him. She quickly ran to him. The boys wouldn't dare come close to her now. Upon seeing Black Kettle, the boys turned around, ready to harass someone else.

"Hi, Father," Morning Dove said, throwing the rabbits and turkey on the grass.

The children ran away, startled. Black Kettle leaned against a vacant tepee, arms folded as he looked at the dead animals. Morning Dove knelt down, wiping her hands on the fresh grass, trying to get rid of the dead animal smell.

"I've had my lesson, but Black Beaver never showed up — he was out hunting as you can see." She straightened. "George is here to see you," she added, smiling, glad she'd got her brother in trouble.

"Morning Dove, remember to help Mother with the feast tonight."

"Yes, Father. I have not forgotten."

"Good. Sometimes you're a dreamer and forget things."

"I only daydream about important things."

Black Kettle sighed. George appeared, finally having caught up. He placed the reading books under his arm and shook hands with Black Kettle before heading into the tepee with him.

Morning Dove reluctantly picked up the carcasses and headed back to the family tepee to help with the feast. Her mind wandered. *What did Father mean when he said I was a dreamer? I always do my chores when asked*, she thought to herself. She stopped outside the tepee, staring at the American flag on top, flying high in the whispering wind. She looked at it in awe. She wanted to go and see the Great White Father in Washington like Black Kettle had done. He was so proud of the flag that Colonel Greenwood had given him. It was a gift to keep the peace, and he had informed Black Kettle that no soldier would fire at him if the flag was displayed.

Black Kettle told so many stories about his trip. The

government had invited Black Kettle and his friend Lean Bear to visit Washington. They'd met Abraham Lincoln, who'd given them medals. They had thought the medals signified their friendship with the White Man. That was until cavalry soldiers killed Lean Bear when he went to greet them peacefully.

Morning Dove stared at the flag, imagining what Washington would be like. She stood still, thinking, for a few moments, before she realised her father was right about her being a dreamer. "I better go and see Mother before I start dreaming again," she said to herself, laughing. She found Medicine Woman Later behind the tepee, peeling wild turnips. "I'm here to help with the feast," Morning Dove said loudly.

Medicine Woman Later jumped, nicking her finger with the knife as Morning Dove sat down beside her, throwing the meat on the ground.

"I have been waiting for you. Where have you been?" said Medicine Woman Later, wrapping her thumb around her finger to stop the trickle of blood.

"Well, Mama, I have been dreaming again." Morning Dove took over peeling the turnips.

"I hope it hasn't been all day."

"Of course not. I have been learning the White Man's words, but something strange happened when I went to the river after some would-be warriors wrestled me to the ground. Can you believe they did that? Very childish."

"Well, they are young boys. They do things you don't

expect. What were you saying about the river?" Medicine Woman Later asked, concerned.

Morning Dove continued peeling the turnips. "After I was wrestled to the ground, I went to wash my face, which was covered in dust, and when I dipped my hands into the water, I saw a face looking back at me. I couldn't make out who it was as there were ripples in the water, distorting the face. There was no one around me. I was scared and ran back to the village. What could it be? Is trouble coming to me?"

"I am not sure what it could be. It sounds like the spirit world is trying to contact you, to tell you something. You should talk to your father and see what he thinks. You might have to see the medicine man or the elders, they will know, but check with your father first — after we prepare dinner. I don't want you wandering off again because dinner might be over by the time you come back."

"Alright, you have my full attention."

Medicine Woman Later sighed, knowing that wasn't entirely true. "I saw your brother. He told me about going hunting." She pointed to the two rabbits and turkey and held out a knife. "Go and prepare them while I start on the wild onions. Everyone is excited about the feast tonight."

Morning Dove wasn't looking forward to skinning rabbits and pulling feathers out of a turkey, but she knew she had to do it, so she went down to the creek bed and tried to do it as quickly as she could. A short time later, Morning Dove came back to the tepee, holding the turkey and two rabbits.

"Mama, you should be proud of me. Look what I did." Morning Dove said boastfully, holding up the skinned carcasses.

"That is good, Morning Dove. You just need to put the rabbits in a pot and the turkey we will put in a fire pit. Everything is prepared now. We just need to get the cooking done. You can see your father about the vision now, but be quick, the meat will not take long to cook."

"Alright, I will go and find him — and I will remember to come back quickly."

Black Kettle and George had made their way to White Owl's, the medicine man's, tepee, where they were sitting outside, smoking the peace pipe.

"Morning Dove, what brings you here? Is everything alright?" Black Kettle asked as she approached.

"Yes, Father. I wanted to talk to you about something that happened today." She sat down in front of the three men.

"What is it? Can it be spoken in front of White Owl and George?"

"Yes, it is alright if they want to stay. I was down at the creek this afternoon and I was washing my face. In the reflection of the water, I saw this strange face looking back at me, and it even started smiling. It scared me, Father. What does all of this mean?"

Black Kettle looked at White Owl. "What do you think, White Owl? You're the medicine man. What could it mean? I have never heard of this happening before."

White Owl smoked the peace pipe before he answered. "The spirits are trying to speak to you, Morning Dove. They want you to know something. This is a very rare occurrence."

"Why do they want to talk to me? What could they possibly want me to know?" Morning Dove asked, feeling very worried.

"What we must do is go back to the creek and see if the face will show itself again," White Owl said authoritatively.

"We cannot do it now," Black Kettle interrupted, "as the dog soldiers will arrive shortly and we need to greet them before the feast starts. It can wait another day."

Morning Dove nodded, but she really wanted an answer. She wandered back to the family tepee to give her mother a hand before the feast started. As she was approaching the tepee, she heard a loud cheer followed by singing, as the dog soldiers were welcomed.

Morning Dove stopped and took in the atmosphere: the dog soldiers looked amazing in all their finery, and their horses looked as strong and magnificent as their riders. The dog soldiers wore fringed deerskin shirts with intricate beading and scalp locks. They wore leggings that were beaded at the side and breechclouts. Their faces were unpainted and their hair was tied in braids, with eagle feathers dangling down, touching their muscular shoulders. Morning Dove was entranced by how exquisite they looked.

"Morning Dove. Morning Dove. I need your help." Medicine Woman Later called out.

Morning Dove ran to her mother before she got into trouble.

2

Troubled Times?

The feast was commencing. The drums were beating in unison with the beat of everyone's heart: *BA BOM, BA BOM, BA BOM*. The painted half naked dancers were circling in a trance to the drums' beat and the singing, thanking the spirits for their generosity. The fire cauldrons were ablaze in the middle of the village, casting everyone in an orange glow. Black Kettle was in the centre, enjoying the activities, proud of his people. It was times like these that he treasured his people and being Cheyenne, but he knew things could change very quickly and without warning.

It was the year of 1864, and times had changed from when he was a young boy. Not only did they have to watch out for enemy tribes, but now also for the White Man, especially the miners who came to dig up their precious earth to find the yellow metal. He sat mesmerized, enjoying the moment. He stared out into the distant horizon, knowing he would be at the mercy of the Whites sooner rather than later. This was always in the back of his mind.

As the music and the dancing settled, the dog soldiers

trickled into Black Kettle's lodge for storytelling. Others tried to cram in too, with women pushing themselves in so they could be part of it. The lodge was filled with laughter and Black Beaver became the centre of attention.

"Tell us the story again, Black Beaver," cried various tribe members, wanting to laugh again.

"I will, but this is the last time. I was riding my horse on the Smoky Hill trail when I saw smoke coming from the bushes. Of course, I knew it was the White Man — who else would make smoke in the middle of the day. As I was approaching, I saw a White Man bathing in the stream. I could hear him making the White Man's words and thought he had a woman there with him as he was singing and being merry. As I got closer, I could hear splashing and frolicking and, little did I know, he was swimming with his mule." Black Beaver burst out laughing. "He was talking to his mule."

Everyone was in hysterics; their laughter was uncontrollable. Black Beaver continued, "I started shooting arrows over his head, just to scare him. He swam underwater and when he bobbed up again, he frightened the mule and it head butted him, knocking the White Man backwards into the water." Black Beaver laughed again and everyone else followed.

"I ravaged his camp but there was not much there. The White Man ran towards me naked, yelling words I did not understand. He did not seem afraid but kept running towards me and then I slapped him across the face and he started crying, begging for mercy. I thought he was funny so I left him alone." Black Beaver cleared his throat. "The next day while I was out hunting, I went back to tease him a bit more, but the mule was not there. The White Man had a dozen arrows sticking in him. They were Sioux arrows."

"I wonder why the Sioux were over this way," queried Tall Bear, concerned.

"You never know what the Sioux could be up to, they are very fierce and I am glad they are our allies and not our enemies," said Buffalo Star.

"The Sioux were probably looking for White Scalps. There are plenty of Whites looking for the yellow metal," said White Feather.

"There are too many Whites everywhere — once you kill one, more come. Blood will moisten the soil and that is not good. Peace has to be the answer." Black Kettle said with authority.

Suddenly, the leader of the dog soldiers, Red Panther, stood up. "You give into the Whites all the time. You sign treaties, for what? They take our land, they kill us and try to capture our women and children. It is better to die while fighting for our way of life rather than being a prisoner on our own land, begging for some flour, sugar and bacon. You are at the mercy of these people who break their promises and do what they like. You disgust me."

The lodge was in uproar — some were nodding their heads in agreement, while others just sat in silence. Black Kettle stood up to address the crowd. "To fight, to shed blood is not good for the Cheyenne. We must survive. If we were to take arms, many of us wouldn't survive. You cannot stop the White Man. There are many, they are powerful, they have money and build tall buildings. I know this as I have been to see the Great White Father in Washington. The Whites keep pouring into our country, this I know. Don't you think I would rather be free and ride my horse through the prairie without any threats from the White Man. My heart is sad, but it will be broken if the great Southern Cheyenne perish at the hands of war. You cannot stop the Whites, they are endless. Our survival depends on co-operating with them and living the way they tell us to."

"NO! NO!" Red Panther bellowed. "You are our leader, but you have become soft towards them. We need someone who will fight these people to the end. My dog soldiers harass the whites we come across. We will fight to the death to protect our country. We are not scared. We do not want to live on a reservation. We will never accept handouts from the White Man. We will not give up our land. We will keep fighting to be free. If I was put on a reservation I would be broken. If a coyote was captured and put in a cage, it would start to eat its own tail, sending itself crazy. If I was captured I would go crazy like the coyote. My heart is fully Cheyenne, and it is my right to walk upon this earth as I please."

Black Kettle cleared his throat. "By doing this you will leave a trail of destruction. The White Man will punish the innocent bands who keep the peace. They will not care whom they punish. Do you see? You may think you are doing a good thing by making war, but they will take their anger out on the peaceful Indians and ask questions later."

"No, they would come to you because they know you will not fight," Red Panther said, disgusted. "We will not hand over our land, we will keep fighting to be free. I made a promise to myself that I was not going to be like the coyote in the cage, who is unable to roam free where it pleases to hunt or to play. I will not be a prisoner on my own land. To all my fellow Cheyenne, do not become prisoners of the Whites. They will use you to the very core. Come and join our camp if you want to live free. I know my heart is fully Cheyenne and I would never take the White Mans' road."

Black Kettle spoke, saying, "Red Panther, please listen, fighting will not help. The White Man is plentiful, he won't stop. More will come, even if you make war and fight them. The ones you kill will be replaced — you cannot get rid of them. Save yourself Red Panther and your dog soldiers. Don't go down the war path, it is too dangerous. There will be much blood shed."

Red Panther was silent a moment. "I am not scared. I would rather be free as long as I can than be trapped by the White Man's world and obey his rules. I am not going to be a victim. I will fight. They have no regard for us. Why are you on their side?"

"I am not on their side. I am trying to keep the peace and prevent a war. The only way to survive is by the Whites' side, even though we may have to give up our right to walk across our land and our old ways, at least we will be alive to live on mother earth. You don't think my heart is sad to know I have to be at the mercy of the Whites and not run where the wild animals roam? Though my heart is sad I am happy that I will save my people from slaughter. Red Panther, save yourself."

"I cannot and will not live like the White Man. If I die, I will die free. I will not change my mind. I have spoken." Red Panther stormed out.

There was silence in the lodge before chatter broke out.

White Owl stood up to address the crowd. "When I was a small boy we could roam the prairie where we liked — there were no invading Whites. They were happy times. We never had to look over our shoulder. We were free and at peace. Of course, we made war on our enemies, as was part of the Cheyenne tradition. There is much glory and prestige to be earned from fighting our enemies and counting coup, but there is none in fighting the White Man, as they are an inferior race. I have seen many miners come through this part of the country. I have watched from a distance. They are clumsy and dirty, not having washed for months. They are poor riders and cannot shoot straight. They are a very strange race. They cannot take our land, where will we go? I am not leaving my land as I am too many years old now to move, yet I am also too old to fight. What will be will be, but we must protect our women and children."

Buffalo Star rose. "White Owl, you may be too old to fight but our young warriors are strong and we are the mighty Cheyenne. We can win the war over the Whites, they are nothing. I vote for war. If we start now the White Man will be too scared to come and take our land. We must act."

Chatter filled the lodge once more. Black Kettle stood up again. "My fellow Cheyenne, as I have said before, we must stay true to the peace path as much as possible. Please do not start any wars. Everything has settled down now." Black Kettle subdued the crowd, who were nodding with much deliberation. They were satisfied with the discussion and left to go to their own lodges.

3

The Adventure

Morning Dove awoke from a lovely dream. She looked around the family's tepee, but no one was there. She stretched her arms and wriggled her body, shaking off the last remnants of sleep. She would have preferred to have stayed in bed and continued dreaming, but village life was always busy. She stuck her head out of the tepee flap and saw dogs running around barking, women commencing their chores and warriors preparing to go on a buffalo hunt.

She picked out her favourite buckskin dress, with beaded fringes and placed her colourful beaded moccasins on her slender feet. No braids today; she would leave her hair wild and free. She made her way out of the tepee and stood still. Her fellow tribespeople were moving in all directions, making her feel dizzy.

"Morning Dove. Morning Dove," Medicine Woman Later called, while she carried a clay pot towards the tepee to commence her morning cooking. "I need you to fetch some fire wood."

"Morning Dove. Morning Dove. I need you to find

your brother. We need to prepare our horses for the buffalo hunt," said Black Kettle as he swiftly passed them both.

Morning Dove sighed. *Life's too short to have obligations,* she thought to herself. She wanted to start her day with some adventure and have a swim in her favourite watering hole, but that would have to wait.

The herders were hurriedly bringing in the horses from their overnight pasture. Morning Dove saw her favourite buckskin mare, Prairie Moon, who was the colour of the summer prairie grass. She spotted her brother and waved him over. "Black Beaver, Father needs you to prepare for the buffalo hunt," she said once he reached her.

"I was deciding what horse to take. I need something fast and swift," Black Beaver replied.

"Why don't you take Father's white stallion. He could run for miles and keep you out of trouble with the buffalo, if they decide to turn on you."

"Would he let me?"

"I don't see why not, but just in case take an extra horse with you, then if he doesn't allow you to ride his horse you don't have to come back. You should go now. They're preparing for the hunt."

While Morning Dove helped her brother with the horses, she noticed bits of discarded wood through the fields; she gathered them up and held them to her brother, who was now mounted on a pinto pony. "Mother would like this wood for her fire."

"Why are you giving this to me? Why can't you follow

up with your duty? This is women's work. Can you not see that I have my hands full with the horses?"

"You are quite capable with horses and are going in that direction to meet with Father, so it makes sense," she said with a smile.

Black Beaver sighed. "Just wait until you are married."

Black Beaver took the wood, juggling it while he guided the pony and led his 'back up horse', a white stallion. Morning Dove retrieved her own horse, Prairie Moon, and walked beside her brother, just in case all the wood came tumbling down.

"Morning Dove, one day you will get married and will have to bare the burdens. Otherwise your warrior husband will throw all of your belongings out of the tepee and divorce you."

"Very funny. I am not getting married anyway. Father says I don't have to if I don't love anyone."

"But you have so many suitors that want to marry you. White Raven gave Father six ponies for you to be his wife."

"Well, Father said no as he was not suitable for me and would not accept anything until he spoke with me about it."

"But, Morning Dove, you need to accept someone's proposal, unless you want to die alone."

"But my heart doesn't want to accept anyone's proposal."

"Alright, I will leave you be now. I have to go and pray to the spirits and get my horse painted before the buffalo hunt. I will see you later, Morning Dove — keep out of trouble."

Morning Dove separated from Black Beaver, leading

her horse to her tepee, where she tethered her outside. She walked to White Owl's lodge, finding it empty. She could hear him chanting, praying to the Great Spirit to bless the buffalo hunt. Morning Dove would have to wait until he was finished. She sat down by his tepee and closed her eyes, listening to the prayer.

All of a sudden the chanting stopped. She opened her eyes and White Owl was standing in front of her. "White Owl, I was just waiting for you. Can we go back to the creek and see if the spirit comes back?"

White Owl nodded. "But, Morning Dove, it may not come back if I am there as well."

"I don't want to go back by myself."

"Okay, let's make our way to the creek together."

"I am going to chant to the spirits," White Owl said when they arrived at the creek. "When I do this, look into the water and yell out if the face appears. It may or may not work as I have never dealt with this type of thing before. The spirit world will only show itself when it wants to. I cannot force it to happen." He began chanting.

Morning Dove stared into the creek, anticipating the face's appearance. White Owl continued chanting, but nothing happened. Suddenly, the apparition appeared, smiling. "White Owl! It's here."

White Owl stared into the creek, but saw nothing. The face had disappeared as quickly as it had come. "It has gone, Morning Dove, and that is what I thought. It may not want to show itself to anyone but you."

"What do I do now?"

"The only thing I can do is teach you a couple of chants to make it go back to the spirit world when it appears again."

"But I cannot chant. Can we try again, please?"

"Okay, just this once, but I wonder why it appears only at the creek. There must be a reason." White Owl started chanting again and, to Morning Dove's amazement, the face reappeared. She tapped White Owl on the shoulder. The chanting stopped and the apparition showed itself to White Owl.

The face became clearer, revealing a male Indian. His mouth moved slowly, but no words came out. White Owl concentrated on the face's lips, interpreting the words he was mouthing, *I am Buffalo That Walks with Me. The Cheyenne are to walk into troubled times, be careful. Morning Dove, you are very powerful. You are a leader.*

The face vanished, leaving Morning Dove and White Owl staring at one another. "Well, Morning Dove, this is very strange. Did you understand what he was trying to tell us?" Morning Dove shook her head. "He said the Cheyenne are going to face troubled times and that you are a powerful leader. This message must be very important for them to communicate with us. I must pray to the spirits for more information. Don't be afraid, Morning Dove. I will speak to Black Kettle when he returns from the buffalo hunt. Go for that ride you were planning, and if the spirits tell me more, I will let you know."

"How did you know I was going for a ride?"

"I just know."

Morning Dove nodded, feeling amazed and scared by everything. She walked back to her tepee. Her mind was solely on the messages from the spirit world. What was going to happen to the Cheyenne? Why was she chosen to receive these messages? She didn't feel powerful, just confused. She mounted her beloved horse and headed through the village, viewing the beautiful scenery before her: the tall mountains in the background, the fluffy clouds, the ripe prairie grass and the crystal clear river. She turned her head to the side and saw her brother from a distance, still present in the village on Black Kettle's white stallion. She was pleased for her brother. The children were playing and the tribespeople were waiting to wish the warriors luck with the Great Spirit, before sending them off on their hunt.

The women were hard at work cooking, bringing in the firewood and water, and making and tanning hides. Later, they would have to bring in all the meat from the hunt. As a single woman, Morning Dove didn't have many chores, and although she always helped, her life was about having fun. She loved feeling free and wild, like an eagle hovering in the sky.

On a serious note, though, she knew her brother wanted her to accept some of the marriage offers given to her father, but she wasn't interested in any of them and told her father to refuse them all — but one day she would have to accept one.

4

The Prisoner

Morning Dove galloped her horse over the prairie. She always loved her 'horse runs', feeling the wind blow through her hair. She headed for her favourite swimming hole, jumping off Prairie Moon, undressing and slipping into the water, its coldness taking her breath away. She splashed around, feeling so happy that she began singing traditional Cheyenne songs.

Her singing cut off when she heard rustling in the bushes. *Danger!* Her stomach twisted into knots. "Who's there? Who's there?" Morning Dove called out. Silence prevailed. Her stomach twisted even more. "Who's there?" she repeated. Silence prevailed again. "Show yourself now. I demand you show yourself!"

Silence...

Morning Dove started to shiver. She didn't know what to do. She was alone, naked, in danger and her horse was further away than she would have liked. She made her way to the edge of the bank and grabbed her dress. She slipped it on in the water so she wouldn't reveal herself. She was still unsure if she should stay in the water or climb the low bank and run to her horse.

The bushes rustled again, scaring Morning Dove so much she held her breath. Her heart was racing so fast she thought it was going to burst out of her chest. *What should I do? What should I do?*

Silence descended again, and it lasted so long Morning Dove began thinking she'd imagined the rustling, but then she heard footsteps that sounded as though someone was walking backwards. The footsteps were light like an Indians, trained in stealth, not like the heavy footsteps of the White Man.

Morning Dove came to the conclusion that it was one of her tribespeople playing a trick on her. Someone may have seen her come here and hid in the bushes. Morning Dove chuckled. "I feel silly now. This story is going to be told around the campfire tonight. I will be the laughing stock of the whole Cheyenne nation." She laughed again.

Morning Dove was about to leap out of the water when she saw the back of an Indian's head protruding through the bushes, with an unusual feather in his hair. She froze when she saw the feather. No one in her tribe wore a feather like that. She jumped out of the water and ran to Prairie Moon, galloping away to the village. Her horse moved like the wind, and Morning Dove's black satin hair moved in unison.

Morning Dove was approaching her village. In the distance, she saw the warriors moving out for the buffalo hunt. She tried to wave them down before they left the village. A couple of warriors noticed her and stopped, pointing in her direction so the other warriors could see.

Black Kettle rode straight to her with the warriors following. Morning Dove was in a panic trying to reach them as quickly as she could. Prairie Moon was galloping her heart out, feeling the urgency of her rider. She slowed Prairie Moon down to a canter, halting in front of Black Kettle and the warriors.

"I have seen an enemy," Morning Dove blurted out, puffing.

"What?!" Black Kettle exclaimed. "How many warriors?"

"Something happened. No, not exactly happened to me... but something could have. Does that make sense? It was only one enemy."

"You are not making any sense," Black Kettle said "You're rambling like a prairie chicken. Take two deep breaths and start again. There was only one warrior? Just one? That doesn't seem right."

Morning Dove took a deep breath. "I was taking a swim at my favourite swimming hole and I heard someone in the bushes. It was an Indian, and as he turned around I could see his head feather, which was unlike anything I've seen — it definitely wasn't Cheyenne."

"Do you know the tribe?" Black Kettle asked.

"No," Morning Dove admitted, disappointed.

Black Kettle's eyes looked distant; his lips were pursed, and frown lines creased his brow. He'd never made rash decisions, always being wise in his choices. He had his whole tribe to think of. The lone Indian could be from an enemy tribe acting as a scout, and others may follow to make war on the mighty Cheyenne and take their well-bred horses — or their women and children.

Black Kettle turned around to the warriors. "My fellow tribesmen, the buffalo hunt will be disbanded due to an enemy sighting. We need to conduct a search. Red Bull, I ask you to stay behind with some warriors to protect the women and children, and to gather any horses roaming the prairie lands so they are not stolen. We will divide into two groups. Wolf Robe, you are in charge of the second group. Pick your warriors now and you will search west of the village. I will search south. Black Beaver, you will come with me. Morning Dove, go back to your tepee and stay close, no more riding, and inform the village crier of my plan so all the village is informed."

Morning Dove made it back to the village and tied her horse close to her tepee in case something happened and she needed a quick getaway. Her heart was still jumpy when she entered the tepee and told Medicine Woman Later what had happened.

Medicine Woman Later put her hands on Morning Dove's shoulders and spoke gently. "Take a deep breath. Centre yourself. You are all worked up about what happened. You are safe now and the warriors are out looking for this enemy. Your dress is soaked, you need to change. For your own safety you should stay in the tepee until Black Kettle comes back. I will be just outside finishing my beading work."

Morning Dove slipped out of her soaked buckskin dress and changed into her everyday dress, which had little beading. She lay on her buffalo skin rug and tried to calm her racing heart. She thought of Black Kettle. How brave he was — so steady and sure. She closed her eyes and drifted into deep slumber, dreaming of snow-covered mountains overlooking a snow-filled valley. There was something in the distance, gradually coming into focus. It was a stunning palomino horse that had long white plaited braids in its glossy mane. Someone was riding the horse. They were garbed in a long white cape, with a fur trimmed hood hiding their face. As the horse came to a frozen stream, the person pulled their hood off, revealing an Indian man with long black braids wrapped in beaver fur. His eyes were wide with intellect, his lips full and his cheeks rosy. He looked so real in Morning Dove's dream, and spoke to her in a loving way.

"You are to represent your tribe through peace. Love through your heart. Your tribe will follow you. You are a bridge between two. Peace is your power." He vanished.

Morning Dove woke up in disbelief; the spirit world was communicating with her through her dreams. She stared at the tepee wall, completely shocked, not sure what to do. She needed to find White Owl. She ran straight to White Owl's tepee, hoping he was there. "White Owl! White Owl! Are you there?"

The tepee flap opened and White Owl ushered her in. They sat down opposite each other, crossing their legs.

"White Owl, I need your help again. I've had a strange dream today. Weird things seem to be happening to me."

"Weird things? Something else has happened with the spirit world?" White Owl asked, concerned.

"When I dozed off after the incident at the water hole, a dream came to me and it seemed so real — there was snow everywhere. A very handsome man was riding a palomino horse and he said something about me being a bridge between two and peace was my power. What does all of this mean? I feel like the spirit world is following me. It's making me uncomfortable."

"Morning Dove, it sounds as though it was Sweet Medicine. He is a cultural hero among us Cheyenne. He brought the medicine arrows to the Cheyenne nation so we could be all conquering and strong. He is very powerful and what he said is very important to your life. You will start to understand his words, keep them close to your heart and always remember them. Sweet Medicine is your friend. Do not be scared. The spirit world sees you as important to this tribe and wants to give you information."

"Oh no. Is that really true, White Owl? Are they going to annoy me for all of my life?"

"Well, Morning Dove, they will probably show themselves to you when they need to and you cannot stop them. Just embrace them."

Shouting, loud chatter and the sound of barking dogs filled the village. Morning Dove thanked White Owl and hurried from the tepee following the noise of the commotion until she spotted her father. He was back with half of the warriors. A man was running beside Black Kettle's horse, with his hands tied in a large lasso. Morning Dove gasped, recognising the Indian's feather as the same one she'd seen at the water hole. The warriors were coming towards the centre of the village, and a crowd was developing; they were yelling and throwing clumps of dirt and rocks at the Indian prisoner. Black Kettle held up his hand for them to stop, just as the second group of warriors appeared, approaching the village and seeing the prisoner.

"Morning Dove, is this the Indian you saw this morning?" Black Kettle asked.

"I never saw his face, but it looks like the same Indian."

The captured prisoner looked straight into her eyes, pleading for mercy. It sparked something in Morning Dove. She had to turn away as his stare looked straight into her soul.

"Tie this prisoner up, Black Beaver, until I know what to do," Black Kettle ordered.

Black Beaver nodded and enlisted the help of Red Calf Robe. They removed the prisoner, using the lasso to walk him to the far end of village, tying each of his hands to pegs that had been hit into the hard ground, and did the same with his legs.

"He is a Crow Indian. You can tell by the way his hair is turned back in a roll off the forehead and the feather in his hair," Red Calf Robe remarked.

Black Beaver nodded and left the prisoner, who started

singing his death song, letting the spirits know he was coming and preparing for his entry into the afterlife.

Morning Dove couldn't get the prisoner out of her mind. She approached Black Kettle as he was attending to his horse, leading it to the open field where all the other horses were. "Father." Black Kettle turned around. "I have come to talk about the prisoner. What is going to happen to him?"

"I haven't made up my mind on what to do with him yet."

"What are his options? He hasn't done anything and he never hurt me."

"Morning Dove, when you were a little girl you always wanted the best for everyone, whether it be an orphaned baby elk or an enemy. When you were about eleven years old you showed your compassion when a young white boy was found in the prairie grass, who'd lost his family through a Sioux attack. We found him and brought him here. You took him under your wing. You knew he was very scared and you convinced me to set him free to live with his own people. We sent him away with the trader. Do you remember?" Black Kettle said in a heartfelt manner.

"Yes, Father, I remember. I wonder where he is now."

"The prisoner here, Morning Dove, is our enemy. They make war on our people. Crows take our horses and they kill us if they have to."

"But, Father, we do the same to them — it's a never-ending circle. Why can't we let him go in peace?"

"I haven't made a decision yet. I will decide his fate later this morning," Black Kettle said, using his authority.

"The prisoner hasn't had any water or food."

"Do as you wish," Black Kettle said with a sigh.

White Owl approached Black Kettle at the edge of the horse's pasture, after he had seen Morning Dove leave. "Black Kettle, let's talk. This is a nice place to sit." They sat on a small rise, stretching their legs out. White Owl pulled the peace pipe from under his white elk fringed shirt. He lit the pipe and passed it to Black Kettle. "I have seen the apparition that was down at the creek with Morning Dove this morning, before all the trouble. His name was Buffalo That Walks With Me. He said Morning Dove was a leader of her people and that the Cheyenne will face troubled times. I don't really know what it all means, but there must be something on the horizon. I also spoke to the spirits and a vision came to me of yells and screams — I was in the middle of chaos. That is all."

Black Kettle was silent, deep in thought. "What could all this mean? I remember the name Buffalo That Walks With Me. I am sure an enemy killed him by the creek and that is where his spirit resides. It sounds as though they are trying to warn us about something. We must be careful. If you get any more information from the spirits, let me know."

White Owl nodded, and they exchanged a look that said they knew trouble was coming to the Cheyenne.

The sun was beating down on the prisoner, making him sweat profusely. Morning Dove noticed this and went to him with a cool cloth, patting his face and head with it.

The Indian looked at her intently again, making her feel as though he were looking into her soul. Morning Dove felt an intense heat and turned away bashfully.

She left to gather water and food, bringing it back to the prisoner. She slowly poured the water down his throat, with the prisoner almost draining the buffalo-skin pouch.

"I am Morning Dove," Morning Dove communicated in sign language known by various tribes, as she knew the Cheyenne and Crow language were completely different.

Morning Dove noticed how handsome the Indian was. His copper skin was shiny with sweat. His chiselled face gave him a god-like appearance, and his muscles rippled every time he moved. He wore beaded leggings, a breechclout and a cloth jacket he'd most likely obtained from a trader. His charcoal hair was shoulder length and glimmered in the sun.

Morning Dove snapped out of her daze and found the warrior still gazing at her. She raised his head so she could feed him some flat bread — he was very hungry. She continued feeding him until he was satisfied.

Using sign language, she communicated, "Do not be afraid. I will help you."

The Indian nodded.

Morning Dove left to find Black Kettle, while the village was busy preparing for its night activities. She found him outside the family's tepee, fixing the American flag, which the wind had blown off. "Father, do you know yet what is going to happen to the prisoner?"

"Morning Dove, I know you are concerned. As I said

before, I will make my decision in the morning. We are going to move him to the back of the village."

"Please untie him. He has been tied up like a wild animal all day."

"We will make him feel more comfortable for the night," Black Kettle assured her.

The dead of night had arrived and Morning Dove knew what she had to do. She felt it was her duty to free the Indian prisoner so no harm would come to him, after all she was the reason he'd been captured in the first place. She grabbed a buffalo robe and extra food. She approached the prisoner and found him sitting upright in a more comfortable position as Black Kettle had promised. She wrapped the robe around him and used sign language again. "I will help you tonight. Here is some more food. I will come back later." Her body tingled at the sight of his rugged body — he was staring at her again. She didn't want anything to happen to this Indian. Morning Dove left him and returned to her tepee to get some rest before the big escape.

Morning Dove felt butterflies in her stomach when she awoke a short while later. It was still dark, and she knew it was time to put her escape plan into action. She made sure everyone in the tepee was fast asleep before tiptoeing to the tepee's exit, where she poked her head out to make sure no one was around. When Morning Dove saw the village was quiet and empty, she hurried to the tail end of it.

When she reached the prisoner, she found him huddled under the buffalo robe. Morning Dove quickly untied him and in sign language communicated, "Follow me."

She guided him through the back of the village, being careful not to disturb the guards who were watching over the horses and keeping an eye out for enemies. They zigzagged through the hundreds of horses, hiding behind them and keeping their heads down. Once they came to a cluster of trees, Morning Dove felt relieved and communicated which way the Indian should go before asking him, "What is your name?"

"Runs With Antelope is my name. I am Crow. My heart is glad that you have helped me. I am sad that I have to leave you."

Morning Dove's heart skipped a beat and she watched him start to run away, feeling sad she would never see him again. She hurried back to her tepee, finding everyone still asleep. She tiptoed to her buffalo robe and nestled back into it before rolling over to get comfortable. Her heart stuttered when she saw Black Kettle looking at her.

"Morning Dove, where have you been?" Black Kettle whispered, not wanting to wake anyone.

She couldn't believe she'd been caught. She pretended she didn't hear him and hid her head under the buffalo robe. She couldn't get Runs With Antelope out of her mind. *Were these the feelings that you were meant to have when you wanted to marry someone?* she asked herself. But he was an enemy; it could never be, and she would never see him again.

5

Sand Creek

orning Dove and Black Kettle were travelling to Fort Lyon today to confirm if the rumours were true that their friend and commander Major Edward Wynkoop had been replaced. Black Kettle and Major Wynkoop had developed a friendship through their desire to maintain peace on both sides. Delicate, soft snow began falling, embracing their faces, as they mounted their horses. They were rugged up in heavy buffalo robes.

They commenced their journey. Morning Dove was riding Prairie Moon, and Black Kettle was on his special Appaloosa, Wildfire. They chose the mares for this journey as they were sure footed, especially trespassing over snow and mountains.

"What will happen if the rumours are true and our friend Major Wynkoop is gone?" Morning Dove asked Black Kettle.

"I am not sure what we will do, but all reports back have said a new chief is there and he has red eyes. We will just wait and see, but when you interpret what he says make sure it is accurate, as we cannot afford to make any mistakes with him if he is as evil as they say."

"But what if I he uses big words that I can't understand?"

"Trust yourself, Morning Dove. George has taught you well and you know the language better than Black Beaver, which is why I have brought you along, as I need someone I can trust. Sometimes interpreters get their words mixed up and they say different things, and then the soldiers become angry."

Their riding continued through snow-covered terrain, everything looked pure around them, like a winter wonderland. After riding all morning they could finally see glimpses of Fort Lyon, where smoke rose from chimneys. Butterflies filled their stomachs; they were always nervous when dealing with soldiers. A guard was outside the Fort, watching them. He raised his hand for them to stop as they came closer to the entrance.

Morning Dove spoke. "Chief Black Kettle is here to visit the major about important business."

When they entered the fort's grounds, there were four soldiers walking towards them, chatting and laughing. One left quickly to find the major, returning a few minutes later with him. "I am Major Anthony. I have replaced Major Wynkoop. What are you doing here? I have no business with you. I have army business to attend to," he said angrily. The four soldiers gathered behind the major, ready if there was any trouble.

Morning Dove introduced herself. "I am Morning Dove and this is our great chief, Black Kettle, who wishes to speak to you. I will be the interpreter today."

Black Kettle and Morning Dove dismounted their horses. To their surprise, the major didn't offer to take them inside for their discussion and simply stood there, waiting.

"Are you sure you know the English language well enough? I have my own interpreter who is half Cheyenne."

"I am quite capable. Black Kettle wishes me to interpret for him exclusively."

"That is a big word, little lady. A lot of the people around here wouldn't know what it means. Very well, you can start," he said arrogantly.

Black Kettle spoke to Morning Dove in his native tongue and Morning Dove interpreted. "Black Kettle has noticed a lot of soldier activity and he would like to move our camp south of the Arkansas River, taking the warriors away from the soldiers. We are not safe where we are. He is quite worried." Morning Dove felt proud of herself for not letting the major dishearten her, despite trying to unnerve her with his stare.

Major Anthony replied, "That is nonsense. Sand Creek is the right place for you to stay. It is your winter camp and you will be under the protection of the Army of Fort Lyon. I give permission for the warriors to hunt for buffalo until your winter rations are given out."

Morning Dove repeated what he said, but did it slowly so she wouldn't make a mistake, especially for Black Kettle's sake. Black Kettle paused for a moment before replying to Morning Dove.

"All right, we will stay for the winter," Morning Dove translated.

Black Kettle and Morning Dove left after their brief encounter; they didn't want to stay any longer because something didn't feel right. But what was it? They led their horses through the entrance before mounting them and heading back home.

Morning Dove asked, "Did I do alright?"

"I was really impressed with how you talked, Morning Dove," Black Kettle said. "From now on, I will take you with me when we head into the fort again, or when there are treaties to sign."

"I would like that. I enjoyed interpreting, but it reminds me of what Sweet Medicine said about me being the bridge for two worlds. I understand that now. Maybe it is my path."

"I think you might be right," said Black Kettle.

They trudged through the cold snow on horseback, lifting their buffalo robes around their faces to keep the warmth from escaping their bodies. "We will stop shortly to rest the horses and have our pemmican," Black Kettle instructed.

Morning Dove loved her dry buffalo meat, especially when it was pounded with extra wild berries, giving it a sweetness she enjoyed.

The journey back to Sand Creek was slow and freezing, but Morning Dove always thought of Sweet Medicine whenever she travelled through the snow because it reminded her of the dream. She felt at peace thinking about him, and knew he protected her. "Isn't the snow so pretty? It's like being in another world. It is so pure and magical."

"Yes, Morning Dove, it is, but it is so cold. My favourite season is spring when everything is reborn again — the flowers bloom, the buffalo become stronger and fatter, and me as well. The streams flow with the melted snow, and the prairie grass grows, providing nutrients for our wild animal friends. Mother Earth lets us live off the land by providing for us so the Cheyenne can prosper. I love our land and what it has to offer." All of a sudden, a snow owl darted in and out of the upcoming bushes, squawking loudly. Black Kettle and Morning Dove stopped in their tracks and silently looked at each other, knowing this wasn't a good sign.

"We must keep moving," Black Kettle insisted.

The owl kept following them on their journey. It was unnerving. They felt very skittish and their eyes darted about.

"What does this mean?" Morning Dove asked. "I'm getting scared. The owl is trying to tell us something, it won't stop squawking. Is something bad going to happen?"

"I don't know what it's trying to tell us. We just need to make it back to our village safely."

"The spirit world seems to be on a sequence. It keeps presenting to me. Firstly, with the face in the creek, then Sweet Medicine, and now this owl. Surely something is not right. Maybe it has something to do with that lone Indian you captured — maybe there is going to be an enemy raid on the Cheyenne," said Morning Dove in a panic, fiddling with her buffalo robe.

"Enough of that talk, Morning Dove. You are making

me scared as well. Since the time the Cheyenne first walked this earth, we have always had warring tribes that tried to steal our horses, women and children, so I don't think that is it."

They continued on their journey and eventually made it back home, thankfully finding their village in good order.

The next morning, Black Kettle woke early; the birds were starting to sing their merry song in the wintery snow, while snowflakes drifted over the village. The snow made everything look pure, fresh and new.

Black Kettle made his way out of the warmth of his tepee and into the freezing cold. The cold nipping breeze took his breath away. He wrapped himself up in his buffalo robe and walked around the village. There were a few women who had the same idea, starting to prepare for the day. They noticed Black Kettle and smiled when he walked passed. He had a gnawing sensation in his stomach that was making him feel uneasy, especially after White Owl's predictions and seeing a snow owl. That was a bad omen.

He was concerned about the White Man's encroachment onto Cheyenne land. He signed many treaties to keep the peace and he knew he was losing some of his followers from the tribe, especially the young warriors who were joining the dog soldiers' camps. That was always on his mind, but he could feel that something unsavoury was coming the Cheyenne's way. He could feel it in his bones.

A flock of ravens flew overhead, squawking loudly. Black Kettle felt nervous. He looked out at the horizon but there was nothing there. He turned around and went back to his tepee where he found the young warrior Jumps With Bears standing outside with five pinto ponies.

"Black Kettle, I am offering these horses for Morning Dove."

"You are only offering five horses?"

"They are five of the best that I have. Tell Morning Dove I have come for her."

Black Kettle dismissed the warrior. Jumps With Bears face fell and he led the horses away, releasing them into the snow-covered prairie lands.

Black Kettle went inside his tepee and lay on his buffalo robe, wondering why he was feeling nervous. He closed his eyes, trying to think of good memories. He saw himself as a young boy happily playing in the water. He saw his father teaching him to ride. The prairie grass was plentiful with roaming buffalo, covering the entire prairie. He saw himself riding the open fields. His mother's face appeared, smiling, calling his name. "Black Kettle. Black Kettle. Be Careful. Be Careful." He woke up, knowing he needed to circle the village's perimeter again. He ventured from his tepee once more, making his way towards the centre of the village, his feet crunching on the crusty snow.

Most of the warriors were not here as they were hunting buffalo. Two thirds of the camp were occupied by women and children. The rest were young boys, the elderly and some warriors who stayed behind. In total, Black Kettle was responsible for six hundred Cheyenne.

Suddenly, a woman came running towards him, yelling, "Soldiers! Soldiers!" She was frantic.

Black Kettle stopped in his tracks, with a sunken feeling in his stomach. He looked towards the horizon and noticed hundreds of blue coats and brown horses. *Yes, it's the soldiers*, he said to himself. *They must be passing through, chasing other rogue bands. They know we are peaceful.*

The village was frantic upon hearing the woman's cries and Indians scurried from their tepees. They spotted the soldiers and started panicking.

Just over seven hundred soldiers turned towards Black Kettle's village, and that's when he knew it wasn't a friendly visit. "White soldiers are coming! White soldiers! White soldiers!" Black Kettle bellowed, warning the other Indians. He grabbed the longest lodge pole he could find and quickly attached his precious American flag to it, along with a white piece of cloth to symbolise peace, so the soldiers would see the Cheyenne were their friends.

Black Kettle, Medicine Woman Later and some of his followers stayed near the flag pole, putting their hands on the pole, conveying they were peaceful. The soldiers hadn't entered the village yet, but the sound of the horses' hooves squelching in the snow and the clang of the soldiers' sabres were getting closer.

The village was in uproar, with people yelling, children crying and the remaining warriors gathering weapons and horses. Black Beaver and Morning Dove were still in the family's tepee. Black Beaver lifted the tepee's flap, seeing all the commotion. He turned to Morning Dove. "Go and save yourself. Go to the sand bank. Go now! Soldiers are coming."

Just as Black Beaver had spoken, the soldiers roared and galloped into the village. Morning Dove fled as fast as her legs could take her. Black Beaver grabbed his rifle and ran towards the other warriors to help.

The soldiers yelled and fired their pistols. Women ran for their lives, carrying their children, while the warriors used their guns and arrows to try and stop the soldiers. Bullets were flying fast, killing anyone who got in their path — not even children were spared. Screams filled the air.

Black Kettle, Medicine Woman Later and his followers at the pole disbanded, running for safety. Black Kettle saw Chief White Antelope walking towards the soldiers, waving his hands to stop the bloodshed. Black Kettle saw what he was doing and yelled, "Come back now. Run, White Antelope!" Just after he said those words, a shower of bullets pummelled into his friend. The soldiers bent down and scalped him while others continued firing at the fleeing Indians — there was no mercy.

The Cheyenne warriors, including Black Beaver, made a desperate flight to the creek bed banks, two miles from the village. The soldiers followed them and hailed them with bullets. Whoever made it to the creek started digging into the loose sand to get cover, and used driftwood for protection. The warriors rallied and tried to organise a defence to protect the women and children.

Black Kettle grabbed his wife and frantically tried to

make it to the creek bed. They had to zigzag between dead and wounded bodies, and through the fierce bullets. Suddenly, Medicine Woman Later was struck down. Black Kettle leant down to help her, but she wasn't moving and blood was oozing from various bullet wounds. Tears welled in his eyes and froze as they trickled down his cheeks. He knew he had to keep moving or the same fate would befall him. He ran as fast as he could and made it to the creek bed where everyone was digging into the snow for protection.

Morning Dove ran to him, shaking. "Father! Father! Are you alright? Where is Mother?"

Black Kettle didn't say anything. He just stared into her eyes and that said everything that words could never express. Morning Dove could see his soul broken and shattered. She started crying. Black Kettle spoke softly, "Stay with your brother. Keep close to the ground, he will look after you. I must rally my people."

"I just want to stay with you, Father," Morning Dove replied, still shaking and crying.

"My sweet girl, it is not safe for you to be with me. You need to stay alive. Go to Black Beaver and stay together."

Morning Dove and Black Kettle stared into each other's eyes for a moment, understanding what each other was thinking; it was a very spiritual moment. Morning Dove quickly left, not knowing if she would see her true hero again.

Black Kettle watched on in horror as soldiers rampaged the village, mutilating and clubbing the dead and wounded, laughing as if in a blood-thirsty trance. No one stood a chance in their path, not even pregnant mothers who had their babies carved from their stomachs. There was nothing anyone could do; the soldiers were just too powerful and wicked. Black Kettle had to turn away. His heart couldn't stand it anymore and he didn't understand why this was happening. They had done everything possible to keep peace with the Whites.

6

The Trek

At sundown, the soldiers ended the battle and began looting the village, destroying it and setting it on fire. The Cheyenne were still too scared to move at first, in case the soldiers came back, and they knew they were in a precarious position where the soldiers could easily storm their defence. Eventually they retreated up the creek. Black Kettle decided he must go back to find his wife's body.

He approached Black Beaver. "I am going back to find my wife. Start making your way along the creek bed. I will catch up."

"If you must, but be careful, the soldiers are all around the village. I cannot tell a chief what to do, especially one who is like a father to me. Morning Dove is comforting an elder who has been wounded. I won't tell her till later as she will become frantic. I will gather the rest of the people and head along the creek, some have already started."

Black Kettle nodded at Black Beaver, grateful he did not talk him out of finding Medicine Woman Later. He was scared of what he may find and knew he had to be extra careful with all the soldiers around. He struggled, making his way through the bodies strewn over the icy ground.

He went back to where Medicine Woman Later had fallen and found her untouched. He scooped her up and heard her moan. *She's alive! She's alive!* The freezing temperatures had sealed off her wounds, stopping her from bleeding to death. Black Kettle carried her back and made his way along the creek. He could see the rest of his people from a distance. They weren't far away, trudging through the snow ever so slowly. Black Kettle finally made it to his people, who halted when they saw him. Morning Dove ran to him.

"Is she alive?" she asked, nodding to Medicine Woman Later.

"Yes, but only just. We must keep moving. The soldiers may catch up to us." Black Kettle led his tribe along the creek in the cover of darkness. He carried his wife with the help of Black Beaver.

Morning Dove kept behind, helping a warrior, who had bullets riddled through his left leg, to walk. The capable tribe members helped the wounded, either carrying them or supporting them as they walked — it was a slow and arduous journey. Most were in pain and could feel the cold nipping to the core of their bodies.

They kept walking along the creek, not sure where they were going, and rested where Black Kettle saw fit. They tended to the wounded during these rest times. Black Kettle knew by instinct that they couldn't stay still for long as they would freeze to death in the open. It was pitch black, but they had to keep moving and try to make it to the dog soldiers' camp on the Smoky Hill River, fifty miles or so from where they were, or find their own warriors who were out on a hunting expedition or finding other allied tribes to help them. Their suffering was extreme and everyone relied on each other to get themselves through this nightmare.

Through hours and hours of darkness, a gradual lightness developed. The morning was approaching; an early ray of sunshine protruded from the sky, illuminating the Cheyenne — an encouragement of hope from The Great Spirit. Suddenly, from a distance, they could see mounted horseman approaching. They weren't sure who they were at first, but as they came closer, they recognised the dog soldiers with food, horses and buffalo robes. One of the Cheyenne warriors had ridden to the dog soldier's camp when the army was approaching, to get help.

Black Kettle couldn't believe his eyes. Food was handed out, and buffalo robes were given to the wounded, taking the chill from their frozen bodies. There weren't enough horses for everyone so they took turns in riding and walking back to the dog soldiers' camp, situated in a hidden valley, surrounded by hilly terrain. For now, the Cheyenne felt safe and would stay there to recuperate. The wounded were looked after as well as could be, but some passed on to the spirit world, their bodies too injured.

The Cheyenne camp at Sand Creek was destroyed. Hundreds of bodies, mainly women and children, were frozen along a trail of destruction. They were now with The Great Spirit.

Morning Dove tended to the wounded while they were with the dog soldiers, making sure they were comfortable and warm. She checked on Medicine Woman Later who was in a tepee with the other wounded. "Mama, you are getting stronger and better each day. Your wounds are slowly healing. You will be alright. The Great Spirit will make sure of that. Our losses have been so great, we will have to start all over again and pray to Mother Earth to replenish us with goodness. Oh, Mama, I am so glad that you're alive. The spirit world was trying to tell us something before this slaughter happened. We should have been more prepared. We should have left Sand Creek, but the soldier chief told us he would protect us. Why does the White Man lie?"

"Morning Dove, you weren't to know of this happening. Even if the spirit world was trying to warn you, you still wouldn't have known about this ambush. Do not blame yourself. We were surprised by the soldiers and did not think they would hurt us, as we took the peace road with the Whites and trusted what the soldier chief at the fort told us."

"But, Mama, I feel as though I could have prevented it somehow."

"No, Morning Dove, do not blame yourself. The spirit world didn't give you enough information to truly know how to prevent it. It is like the time when White Owl had a vision about seeing chaos around him, but he didn't know what it meant, and even with this information, he could not prevent it."

"I see your point, Mama."

The weeks went by and seemed to linger on. The wounded
had recovered, the snow was starting to melt and the bit-
terness of the cold was subdued. It was time to start over
again. The Southern Cheyenne were divided in their loy-
alties — to follow Black Kettle or to go on the war path.
Black Kettle knew in his heart that he had lost many of
his followers, but he would never go to war. He knew better. His heart was heavy with the knowledge that they
would have to find a new residence. They could never go
back to their old hunting grounds; the soldiers had taken
their land, so now the Cheyenne would have to push further south, below the Arkansas joining the Southern
Arapaho, Kiowa and the Comanche.

Some of the dog soldiers went back to Sand Creek to
herd the Cheyenne's horses. To their surprise, they only
found half of the original herd. They suspected the others were rounded up by the army. They were disgusted by
what they saw before them. The village had been burnt
to nothing; feelings of revenge and the desire to create
havoc burned inside them. They returned to their camp,
giving the horses back to Black Kettle.

Many of the warriors were now contemplating their
future with Black Kettle. Being in a dog soldier camp,
they were influenced by their stance with the army and
settlers. After what they saw at Sand Creek, most of them
didn't want to be peaceful now. They were angry.

The time had come to leave the dog soldiers' camp.
Black Kettle felt dejected and drifted off with four hundred followers southbound. He led them on horseback,

with Morning Dove, Black Beaver and Medicine Woman Later riding at the front with him.

Morning Dove commented, "Father, do not blame yourself with what has happened. We weren't to know. You could not have stopped it. The soldier chief lied to us, pretending that we were safe. I had a good talk to Mother about how I thought I could stop it myself, after all the spirits were trying to tell me something, if only I had paid more attention, but it just couldn't be predicted — the when or how. It was out of our control. You are still someone who I look up to, someone I aspire to be like."

"Thank you for your kind words, Morning Dove. We have been decimated and have to start over again. I have lost many of our warriors to the dog soldier's leader, Leg In The Water. I cannot stop them. I can only do the best for the people who want to follow me. Although my heart is broken, we will continue, we need to for the sake of our Southern Cheyenne band."

On hearing this, Black Beaver stopped, and turned to his father. "I cannot do this, Father. Please do not be angry, but I must go with our warriors and join the dog soldiers. I need to do this. Please don't talk me out of this. And please don't worry, I heard from a dog soldier that George Bent is going with his wife and sons, so I will be in good company."

"Black Beaver, you are the son I never had, we are connected like a father and son should be. You are old enough to do as you please and be responsible for your actions, but please be careful. I know you are going on the war path, and I cannot prevent that. The warriors have lost faith in me."

"Oh, Father, I haven't lost faith in you. Not all of the warriors were there at the time of the tragedy. I saw everything with my own eyes. If I don't go and fight, I could never be the strong and fearless warrior I need to be, and I will regret it, and the warriors would never let me forget about it."

Black Kettle looked into Black Beaver's eyes, saying nothing, allowing their souls to meet in understanding. Tears welled in Morning Dove's eyes; she dreaded what may happen to her brother but she had to let him go. They said their goodbyes and went their separate ways.

The dog soldiers and the Southern Cheyenne warriors went north and blended with their northern allies. The Northern Cheyenne looked wild compared to the Southerners, as the Southerner's had contact with traders and Whites who supplied them with cloth blankets and leggings. The gathering of the Sioux, Northern Arapaho's and the Cheyenne vowed revenge for the massacre at Sand Creek. War was being planned — they were smoking their war pipes, cleansing away evil and bringing protection from The Great Spirit. There was much feasting and celebrations, as the beat of the war drums was here.

Raids along the South Platte commenced, wagon trains, stage stations, and military forts were attacked and the town of Julesburg burned. Food shortages began to grow throughout the vicinity. The settlers grew increasingly worried.

1

Clinton McKay

C linton McKay looked out from his bedroom window in Ann Arbor, Michigan. He was grateful for what he saw and heard: the beautiful blue aqua sky with white cottonwool clouds, the greenness of the valley, the harmony of birds singing and the laughter of his two nieces, Grace and Barbara, trying to give their new puppy, Mable, a bath. Clinton chuckled as Mable jumped out of the silver wash basin and shook herself all over the children. The children, completely soaked, ran after her, giggling.

Their mother, Charlotte, who was attending to her vegetable patch, laughed with them before making her way into the house to grab towels for the drenched crew outside.

"Is everything okay?" Charlotte asked Clinton, noticing his distant stare.

"Yes, I'm fine," Clinton reassured her, scratching his head of blond hair.

His sister had been through so much after losing her husband, John, in the Civil War a year ago: raising two children and struggling financially every day. What money she did have went towards repairs on her cottage, which had been damaged in a kitchen fire. It was still liveable, but there were wooden boards that needed replacing in the kitchen. She had no other family members around her, and Clinton knew she felt alone, often crying herself to sleep, where she had nightmares about him befalling the same fate as her husband.

Clinton's nieces were growing up fast. Grace, who had just turned seven, looked like Charlotte, with brownish-blonde hair that flowed in loose wavy curls, and mesmerising light green eyes. Barbara, on the other hand, looked just like her father, with straight short dark hair, dark eyes and delicate features. She was only four but had the mannerisms of her father, such as putting her hands on her hips when she didn't get her own way.

Clinton was glad he was here to ease his sister's burden. While fighting in the Civil War he had often thought of her to keep him going. He had seen things that no one should ever see. His mind was still in the Civil War; sometimes he would wake up from nightmares hearing the screams of wounded men and the zing of bullets tearing into human flesh. He would close his eyes and try to think of nice memories, but instead he would see men with one leg or one arm, walking around with a glazed look upon their faces. Looking outside his window, and seeing these beautiful scenes, made him feel grateful to be there.

The Civil War consumed his life still. It had been three months since he'd returned home, and he knew he had to give himself time to adjust back to normalcy. He was used to living day to day, seeing death often, sleeping and living in the open with gunshots all around him, just trying to survive.

Clinton made his way out to the small back porch and leant back in the wooden rocking chair. He chuckled again when he saw his nieces still trying to catch Mable.

"Clinton, we need your help," yelled Charlotte.

Clinton made his way over to the hysteria. He managed to catch Mable and handed her to Charlotte, all wet and smelly. Then Clinton caught Grace and Barbara and the three of them fell to the ground in fits of laughter, tickling each other.

"Stop it, Uncle Clint. I can't take it anymore," Grace said, laughing.

"Come on now. We better get you all dry." Charlotte threw the towels at Clinton while holding Mable. "Girls, we need to go inside and change before you catch a cold. Hurry up now. Clinton, I will give you the pup. Dry her down and then take her to the shed."

"Yes, ma'am." Clinton took the puppy and dried her off.

"Oh, and Clinton, remember to do the repairs on the front door. When John comes home, he will be really impressed that he won't have to fix it."

"Sis, do you realise what you just said?" Clinton placed the puppy in the shed and came back to focus on Charlotte.

Tears welled in Charlotte's eyes and her lips trembled. She took a few minutes to compose herself. "I keep wishing and hoping he'll walk through the gate. I still remember the day my heart broke in two, beyond repair.

I was so alone. I'm so glad you are here with me now. We need you so much, Clint."

Clinton hugged Charlotte, holding on to her tight. "Sis, you will be okay. I'll make sure of that. You have made it this far. John would be proud."

Charlotte nodded and headed inside to attend to the girls. One thing Clinton knew for sure was this was where he was meant to be.

"Hello, anyone home?" a voice called from the front porch. Clinton turned around and couldn't believe his eyes. It was Tom Custer, one of his friends from the Civil War.

"Oh my, Tom. I can't believe you're here. How did you find me?"

"I knew you were in Ann Arbor somewhere, so I just asked around and an elderly couple told me you were here with your sister."

"It's good to see you. You look well." Clinton embraced Tom.

"I'm staying with my family in New Rumley, Ohio, and they've been fattening me up. Now it's time to see my half-sister, Lydia, and her husband, David, back in Monroe, and I thought since I'm in Michigan, I should look you up."

"We were both skin and bones when the Civil War ended," Clinton remarked.

"Yes, we were, but you're looking good now yourself — your blue eyes are practically sparkling." He laughed.

"Come on in, Tom. I'll introduce you to my family." They stepped into the house. "Charlotte, come and meet one of my good friends," called Clinton.

Charlotte appeared from one of the rooms.

"Charlotte, this is Tom Custer, from my Civil War days."

Charlotte smiled warmly. "It's nice to meet one of Clinton's friends."

"Nice to meet you, Miss Charlotte. Clinton has told me a lot about you. I feel like I know you already," Tom said courteously.

Barbara and Grace appeared beside Charlotte, still in their wet clothes.

"And these two little munchkins are my nieces Barbara and Grace," Clinton introduced them. "They've been up to mischief again with their new puppy, hence why they're a little wet. You girls need to finish changing into some dry clothes. Off you go now." They scampered towards their rooms. "Tom, why don't we sit out on the porch and catch up on news."

"I'd like that very much."

"It's still a pleasant afternoon. I'll bring some coffee and biscuits out," Charlotte offered, her eyes lingering on Tom.

Clinton and Tom made their way onto the porch and sat on the two wooden rocking chairs.

"So, Clinton, what have you been up to since the war finished?" Tom was wriggling from side to side, trying to get comfortable. "It's hard to believe that peace was finally declared this year — 1865 will be a year to remember," commented Tom.

"Yes, I know," Clinton agreed. "I've been recovering, getting myself together. I'm here with Charlotte now and her two daughters. She lost her husband a year ago, so I'm helping her for the moment. We've been living off my life savings so far, but I'll need to find a job soon. How about you?"

Charlotte interrupted. "Excuse me, gentlemen, I've made some coffee and my special jam drop biscuits — the girls favourite."

"Much obliged, Miss Charlotte," said Tom.

"Thank you, sis." Clinton reached for the small stool beside him and placed it between him and Tom. Charlotte placed the tray on the stool and headed back inside.

Tom took one of the coffee cups and began sipping. "I've been with my parents as well as my sister, Margaret, and my three brothers, Nevin, George and Boston — we've been having fun as we always do, playing practical jokes. George's wife, Libby, has also spent some time with us. George did very well for himself during the war. He's known as the boy general now. Mother and Father are so pleased to have both their sons home in one piece — maybe that's an understatement, as when Mother saw me she wept and, surprisingly, so did Father."

Clinton nodded and bit into a jam biscuit. "It had a great impact on family, the dreaded war. It's been a long one for us and our families."

"Yes, it's certainly tested every man, woman and child. But I'll tell you what, Clinton, I'm starting to get itchy feet."

"My feet aren't itchy yet," Clinton said. "I know I have to prepare for the future, but I'm content to just be here for the moment. It's good to spend time with Charlotte and the girls. They would be all alone otherwise. Sometimes the adjustment from war to civilian life is difficult, but I'm loving it out here in the quiet — it's good for the mind. You're welcome to stay, Tom, so you don't have to travel back tonight."

"Thank you, Clinton, I'll welcome that offer. It'll be good to catch up and be with a friendly face."

Clinton pushed to his feet. "I'll be back in a minute. I'll inform Charlotte you're staying." Clinton returned a few minutes later, finding Tom had polished off the last of the biscuits. "Charlotte is going to make up the spare bed."

"Thank you, Clinton. Much obliged."

Hours passed with Clinton and Tom laughing and reminiscing. "Tom, I'm just going to the garden to pick some vegetables for tonight. Follow me and we will chat some more." They walked down the porch steps and turned left, finding a small, blooming vegetable garden.

"You're really getting domesticated now, aren't you, Clint?" Tom remarked, following Clint into the garden.

"I suppose I am. I try and give Charlotte a hand as much as possible." Clinton bent down and pulled out a bunch of carrots, handing them to Tom.

"You will make a good husband someday — if I was a lady, I would probably marry you."

"Gee, Tom, I just don't know what to say about that, but I'll keep that in mind if I don't find that special lady sometime soon," said Clinton, picking ripe tomatoes.

"There are plenty of ladies out there, you just need to mingle," said Tom taking the tomatoes from Clinton.

"I bet you know all about that. You're a charmer, Tom. The ladies fall at your feet." Clinton grabbed the small pitchfork laying nearby and started unearthing onions.

"I don't know if they *fall* at my feet, but they do come running — especially when I'm in uniform."

Clinton balanced the onions on top of the tomatoes and carrots in Tom's hands. "So, have you been seeing anyone since you got back?" Clinton wiped his dirt covered hands on his trousers.

"Well, yes," admitted Tom sheepishly.

"Come on, don't get coy with me. You have to tell me. Hold that thought. I'm just going to find a basket to put the vegetables in. I should have done that before we started. You are looking a bit overloaded there, Tom."

"Yes, I am. I'll wait right here because if I move, everything is going to tumble."

Clinton rushed off to get a cane basket from the kitchen before returning to Tom, who unloaded the vegetables into it.

"Okay, let's get back to important things — the women in your life," said Clinton.

"Mary-Beth Swanson," Tom finally admitted. "A nice English girl. And then Angie — she's such an angel and looks like one too. And then I caught up with Kate, an old friend of mine."

Clint gaped. "You've been seeing three girls at once?"

"I wouldn't put it that way — I saw them at *separate* times. The war has been long and hard and I haven't touched a woman for so long. I'm just making up for lost time. I'm not hurting anyone, and these women know it's causal. They're just in love with the uniform and what it brings," Tom said while scratching his neck with his dirty hands.

"Very well, if that's what you want, but I can't even find one date. What have you got that I don't?"

Tom rubbed his chin. "Hmm, let's see... maybe it's irresistible charm — and I've got special moves women love." He winked. "But in all seriousness, you just have to mingle, Clint."

"I don't think I have the moves or charm, and I also don't have two congressional medals for show and tell — by the way, congratulations on receiving those medals, not one but two. You Custer brothers seem to flourish in war, your bravery just shines."

"Thank you for those kind words. Yes, it was an honour to receive the medals, but, Clint, you don't need them to find women — although it helps to get that special attention. You have charm though, and you're a decent, good man. What else could a woman want? One day I will introduce you to some women."

"Hopefully not your leftovers."

"No, only the best for you, my friend."

"Come on, let's get these to Charlotte." Clinton nodded his head to the basket of vegetables. "She's a really good cook. She'll make a good wife for someone."

"What are you implying? That we would be a good match?" Tom asked, following Clinton back to the cottage.

"Well, yes. I saw her looking at you. She deserves to be happy."

"I'm not ready to settle down yet, and I don't think she's ready either — she's suffered a loss that only time can heal."

"Well, it was worth a try, you never know what may happen. You both could fall madly in love with each other." Clinton grinned, wandering into the cottage with Tom.

"Cut it out," Tom hissed, both ending up at the small kitchen, where they found Charlotte kneading dough with flour in her hair and on her face. "Sis, you are vigorously pounding that dough and you're covered in flour," observed Clinton.

Charlotte smirked and continued kneading. "What have you gathered for supper?"

"We've brought you some carrots, tomatoes and onions." Clinton put the basket on the table. "I'm sure Tom will give you a hand."

"Can you, Tom?" Charlotte smiled warmly at him, wiping her flour coated hands on her apron. "You can start by washing the vegetables and cutting them up."

"I can do that for you. I am at your service Miss Charlotte," Tom said, shooting a grinning Clint a reproachful look.

Tom was in the kitchen while Clinton was setting the table in the supper room, and Charlotte was checking on the girls. Clinton walked into the kitchen in a jovial mood. "While you are helping Charlotte in the kitchen, Tom, sparks might fly, and I'm not talking about the wood burning stove." He winked.

Tom rolled his eyes. "Very funny, Clinton." He finished chopping the vegetables and left them on the chopping board. Clinton started laughing as he went back to finish setting the table.

As Charlotte was entering the kitchen she asked, "What is so funny? I can hear laughter."

"Never mind, Miss Charlotte, your brother just thinks he is funny."

"Yes, that's my brother." Charlotte began breaking up the dough, moulding it into small bread rolls. "I see you have finished preparing the vegetables. Do you mind heating the stove and then cooking the vegetables in that cast-iron pot?" She pointed to the pot. "There is already wood in the stove."

"Yes, ma'am," Tom said obligingly and got to work on the stove.

"So, Mr Custer what do you think you will do now that the war is over?"

"I think I will stay in the army. There is something that takes your soul when you are at war, and when you come back to a normal civilian life it doesn't feel right. Your soul craves the dangers and all that it brings with it."

"Oh! You could always try something different, and you never know, it could take those cravings away, setting you free. It could even lead you in the direction of finding that special someone and starting a family. To me that sounds better than returning to the army. Don't endanger your life, Tom."

"Thank you for your concern, but I think army life is in my blood — I suppose we will see."

Charlotte and Tom continued talking as they finished their tasks. "Thank you for your help," Charlotte said once the bread rolls were in the oven and the vegetables cooked. "Those vegetables smell delicious. I am going to make soup. I have a recipe that was handed down from my grandmother many years ago. I will finish off now, Tom."

Tom handed Charlotte the wooden spoon he'd been using. "It was my pleasure. Thank you for your hospitality — everything smells great."

Tom headed into the reading room where Clinton was sitting in a rocking chair with overstuffed pillows. Tom sat opposite him, on an antique chair. They relished their time together and continued their banter.

Forty minutes later, Charlotte made her way to the supper room. She placed a large bowl of her special soup in the middle of the table and a tray of roasted carrots with her bread rolls, which smelt divine.

"Barbara. Grace. Time for supper," Charlotte called.

The girls came running and plonked themselves on the timber chairs surrounding the timber table. Clinton and Tom joined the girls, with Charlotte sitting at the head of the table.

"Let's say grace and give thanks." They all bowed their heads and Charlotte spoke a simple prayer. "Dear Lord, thank you for giving us what we have today — family, friends and laughter and food on the table. Amen."

"Amen," everyone said in unison before tucking into their supper. There was silence, apart from the clinking of cutlery and the girls giggling as they made funny faces at each other.

"Girls, stop your giggling and finish your supper. Otherwise Uncle Clinton won't tell you a bedtime story," Charlotte rebuked them.

"Yes, Mama," they both said.

"Yes, that's right, girls, no bedtime stories if you don't behave," Clinton said. "Have I told you the story about the uncle who turned into a wolf and ate his nieces because they didn't finish their meal?"

The girls looked at him uneasily. Then with a roar, Clinton reached over and grabbed them. There was so much giggling and laughter.

8

The Friend and the Future

Charlotte flopped in the rocking chair in the living area, leaving Clinton to entertain the children with a bedtime story. She could still hear Tom putting away the dishes, but couldn't move to help him as she was exhausted after a long day. She undid her bun, releasing her bouncy curls, and tossed her hair back. Tom walked in and sat on the antique chair opposite Charlotte. She noticed Tom staring at her, his eyes mesmerised. Charlotte pretended not to notice, but felt her cheeks burn. No man had looked at her that way since John had died.

"Charlotte, next time I will take you out to eat so you don't have to cook... and I will debate whether we will take your brother."

Clinton walked in and feigned offense. "I heard that Tom, you wouldn't just leave me here to cook for myself." Clinton sat down on one of the timber chairs.

"I might. You do need to learn how to make meals. What if you never find a wife? You'll be skin and bones if you can't cook for yourself," Tom said jokingly.

"If I don't find a wife, I'll hire a housekeeper as I just can't cook." Everyone laughed at this.

"Charlotte, you really need to teach your brother some recipes," Tom remarked. "He even makes the worst coffee. I always had to spit it out, and when you are fighting a war, you need a decent cup of coffee. I'll tell you one thing though, it saved me a bullet wound. I had my head down while I was spitting out the worst coffee I had ever tasted, when a bullet from the grey army whizzed past my head. If I hadn't been spitting out that coffee it would've gone straight through my skull."

"Well, I think you owe me one, Tom."

"Yes, I owe you a round of the best whiskey, and then you owe me a double round of whiskey for drinking that damned tasteless mud water. So, I guess we're even." He grinned.

Charlotte pushed to her feet. "I think it's time for me to retire to bed. Don't stay up too late, boys, and try to keep the raucous laughter down. Remember, there are two young girls sleeping and I don't want you waking them."

"We will do our best, Charlotte," Clint said. "We're not too far away from getting some shut eye ourselves."

"You have sweet dreams now, Miss Charlotte," Tom said, "and thank you again for your hospitality."

"It's good having you here. Stay as long as you like," said Charlotte.

Tom smiled. "Thank you. I have enjoyed myself immensely."

Charlotte left, making her way to her bedroom, her cheeks burning again.

"Were you two flirting just then?" Clinton asked. "I have never seen Charlotte be that encouraging to anyone, especially a man."

"A man? I am not just a man, but a man of many talents. Charlotte is coming out of her shell now. Flirting is healthy, Clinton. You should try it sometime and maybe, just maybe, you might find that good cook after all. I still have hope for you, my friend, but don't leave it too late because housekeepers can be pretty expensive — wives are cheaper."

"I know, Tom. I just need to mingle."

"Yes, you do — the sooner the better."

Clinton slouched in his chair and suggested, "Let's have a nightcap. Coffee?"

"Very funny, Clinton." Tom got to his feet. "I will make it so I don't spit it out. Look, listen and learn," he said, leading the way to the kitchen, with Clinton following, "so at least when you start courting, you can make the lady coffee." He started preparing the coffee. "She may starve but at least she'll have something to give her energy."

"My coffee isn't that bad," Clinton argued. "I drink it."

They stayed in the kitchen, sitting on stools, drinking coffee and whiskey, which Clinton had stored away, not letting Charlotte know that he had it in the house. They started talking about the war and eventually their conversation turned sombre and they decided to get some rest — after they hid the whiskey.

They retired to their rooms. Once Clinton's head hit the pillow he was disturbed about what his future held.

He felt he didn't fit in anywhere. He wasn't a farmer, a tradesman, a saloon keeper or a merchant. He was going through his savings and knew he had to make a decision soon on what to do. Maybe, just maybe, his only option was to go back to the army. He spent the night tossing and turning, his mind filled with too many thoughts.

The music of the birds on the following sunny morning inspired Tom to get an early start to the day. He dressed and headed to the porch, breathing in the fresh morning air. He heard someone pottering in the kitchen and headed back into the cottage. It was Charlotte gathering ingredients and pans to prepare breakfast.

"Good morning. Did you sleep well?" asked Charlotte.

"Good morning. I slept like a baby. It is so nice to sleep on a mattress rather than the hard ground I was used to in the war." Tom noticed Charlotte's green eyes were sparkling.

"I'm just making some pancakes for breakfast," Charlotte said.

"I will make the coffee, then," said Tom.

"You don't have to go today. You can stay a bit longer if you like." Her eyes were hopeful.

"That is kind of you, but I need to visit the rest of my family and organise things for my applications to re-join the army, and I have to help my father with a couple of things."

Charlotte's shoulders slumped. "Oh, alright. Well, don't be a stranger. Come and visit us anytime. Clinton loves having you around. I wish you would consider something else besides returning to the army. It is too dangerous."

"It's in my blood now. I cannot step away from it. There is nothing else I want to do. My passion is being a soldier. It is dangerous, but that's what I love — it keeps me on my toes. Life without passion is like not actually living."

"I think I understand now, but I hope Clinton doesn't get the same idea as you."

As if hearing his name, Clinton walked into the kitchen with his nieces. "Good morning, everyone. I found these two wandering in the hallway." He ruffled his nieces' hair. "So, my two little munchkins, let's have some breakfast."

Everyone pulled up the kitchen stools and hovered around the breakfast table. Clinton placed cutlery and plates on the table while Charlotte put a stacked pile of pancakes in the centre, and Tom handed out coffee — water for the girls. Everyone gobbled down the food.

Tom patted his belly after he'd finished his plate. "Thank you, all, for your hospitality. It certainly has been wonderful. I will visit again when I can, but hopefully I'll be able to reenlist as a soldier."

"It has been good seeing you, Tom," said Clinton, rising to his feet along with Tom. He shook Tom's hand and hugged him.

Clinton and Charlotte escorted Tom to the door.

"Thank you again, Miss Charlotte, for everything."

"You are most welcome. Come back soon to visit."

Tom gave Charlotte an admiring glance before departing, leaving Charlotte blushing again.

One week later, Clinton was nervous to speak to Charlotte.

He found her sitting on the porch, mending some of the girls' clothes, while the girls were running around with Mable. This was his chance. He sat down beside his sister and cleared his throat, finding the courage to say what he needed to. "Charlotte, I have been thinking about what my future holds. It wasn't an easy decision by any means. I suppose having Tom visit influenced my decision, and I know you are not going to like it. I need to earn a living."

Charlotte stopped her mending work. "What is it, Clinton? Now you have me worried."

"I have decided to join the army again." Clinton cringed when he said that. "Well, specifically the cavalry. Tom was right, once you get war fever in your veins, it is hard to ignore. I know you don't want me to be a soldier again, but my career options are limited. At least I will get regular pay, even if it's not that much, and most of it will go to supporting yourself and the kids."

Charlotte was speechless.

"Charlotte, please say something — anything. I know you don't want me to re-join the army, and I understand that wholeheartedly, but it is something I have to do. I need to earn a living and this is the way to go about it. I wouldn't be suited to any other occupation. I feel exactly as Tom does in this regard — nothing else fills me with passion."

Charlotte finally found her voice. "Why, Clinton? I don't want anything to happen to you. Being a soldier is so dangerous and I will worry every day, but I cannot stop you if that is what you want to do. I don't want you to be miserable either."

They hugged each other, knowing that soon they would be separated again.

"If you need me for anything just tell me and I will try to get leave to come back. I am going to put my application forth for a position in the cavalry as a lieutenant. I will head down to the telegraph office and organise it there, so hopefully I will hear something in the next couple of weeks. I am sure there is a position out there for me."

"You certainly have made your mind up and you seem excited about it. I just don't understand you men and why you have to put yourselves in danger."

"Sis, I don't think you are meant to understand it. We are cut from a different cloth. That's what Father used to say when Mother did things he didn't agree with."

"Yes, I remember. They were the good old days. I miss them, I really do." Tears swelled in Charlotte's eyes.

"Come on now, don't get teary eyed. You just have to hold on to those memories. They sustain you, they really do. I should know as memories of you and our family is what got me through the war. I will be fine out there, and I promise I won't take any unnecessary risks. If I got through the Civil War, then I can get through this next calling. I will just take it day by day," Clinton said, trying to reassure Charlotte. He knew there was a possibility he may not come back, but he had to take that chance. He just couldn't stay here any longer, or he would end up penniless. He had to take control of his life and face his true destiny.

A month had passed since Clinton put in his application

to join the cavalry. He was at the general store, getting a few things, when a voice called, "Clinton. Clinton." Clinton turned around and saw Joseph, a worker from the telegraph office. "I wanted to catch up with you, Clinton. There is a letter waiting for you. It has been there for a couple of days. It looks important."

"Thanks, Joseph. I was just about to head over and see if there was anything for me."

They both walked over to the telegraph office and Joseph handed him the letter. Clinton ripped it open and smiled when he read it. He rushed back to the cottage, finding Charlotte making cookies in the kitchen. "Charlotte, I have received news. I have been accepted into the cavalry, and I am to report to General Colby at Fort Laramie. I have instructions here on my travel and how to get there. I am to leave within a week."

"Well, I can't say I am happy about the news," said Charlotte, upset.

"Let's not dwell on it. Let's make the most of the time we have left."

Charlotte nodded, liking the idea.

The week passed by, far too quickly. Charlotte was trying to be strong but her heart was breaking inside. The family was out the front of the cottage, saying their goodbyes.

"You two be good for your mama, and make sure you eat your vegetables — and no food fights." Clinton bent down and hugged Grace and Barbara.

"Uncle Clint, I can't breathe you're holding me too tight," gasped Grace. Clinton let them go.

"We will miss you so much, Uncle Clint. We love you," they both cried in unison.

"I love you both so much too. I will think of you always." His gaze turned to Charlotte. "Well, Charlotte, this is it. I will miss you greatly. I told Mr and Mrs Smith next door that I was leaving and to check in on you from time to time. Mr Smith should be here shortly with his horse and cart. He's taking me to town to catch the train. I think they relish having things to do now that all their family has married."

Charlotte nodded, tears streaming down her cheeks. Clinton gave her a big hug, tears running from his eyes as well. He didn't know what was ahead of him; he could only assume that everything would be okay.

9

Fort Laramie

Clinton finally arrived at Fort Laramie; as soon as he had made it through the dusty plains, he was mesmerised by all the colourful and interesting people there. Immigrants were passing through, gathering supplies, attending to stock, and making repairs — they were allowed to stay at the back of the fort, close to the river. One thing that surprised Clinton was the gathering of Indians, all in their colourful headdresses and beaded buckskins. It was like a community.

Clinton felt right at home. He stood still for a moment, not knowing which way to go. He approached a lieutenant walking by, and saluted. "Excuse me, Lieutenant, do you know where I can find General Colby? I am First Lieutenant Clinton McKay. I am to report to him."

"The General is at the stables, inspecting horses. If you go straight down and turn left you should find him. I am First Lieutenant Jacob Smith."

"Good to meet you. There seems to be a lot of activity here today."

"Yes, we have had some Sioux and Northern Cheyenne

come for a peace talk. They have been raiding the Powder River country, harassing immigrants and everyone going up the Bozeman Trail to Montana. Red Cloud has been the mastermind of it all, but of course he never showed up for the peace talks. Don't get too settled here because I think we're heading out in a couple of days, escorting immigrants, stagecoaches and everyone else that wants to get through safely. It is too dangerous to go on the Bozeman Trail in small numbers. There were a couple of miners who ventured out alone. We found them scalped with arrows sticking out of them like a pin cushion. The Indians are mad. I mean really mad."

Clinton stayed silent, wondering what it would be like fighting Indians instead of grey coats. "I better see the general," Clinton said and left Jacob, heading for the stables. When he arrived, instinct told him the general was the man with dark brown shoulder length hair and a full beard. He was inspecting horses in the stables for soundness. "Excuse me, General. General Colby?"

The general turned away from the horse he was inspecting, his eyes focusing on Clinton. "Yes, I am General Colby. What can I do for you?"

Clinton saluted. "I am First Lieutenant Clinton McKay, reporting for duty, sir. Here's my papers." He held them out.

The general scanned the papers and nodded. "Have you had any fighting experience?"

"Yes, sir. I was in the Civil War for three years in the cavalry."

"Good, well at least you know how to handle firearms

and ride a horse. I don't have to train you, which is a bonus as I get a lot of greenhorns that don't speak much English and I waste my time trying to get them ready for life in the army. So, it's good to have you on board. While you are here, we will give you a horse and then go to the army storeroom and get you outfitted before organising a bed at the cavalry barracks."

"Thank you, sir."

"There is a horse here that could be alright for you." The general led Clinton to a horse that was standing at the back of his stall. He was a plain looking brown bay gelding, with no distinctive markings. "He's a sturdy looking thing. An immigrant sold him to us while passing through. He looks like a Clydesdale cross or something — one of those horses that pulls the ploughs on farms. Not the best-looking horse in the outfit, but he has a good strong constitution. He is as tough as an ox the immigrant was saying. So, what do you think?"

Clinton's instincts told him to say, "Yes, I will have him."

"Very well, you can have time to get to know him tomorrow. Right now, we need to get you outfitted and that includes your uniform, ammunition, mess kit, saddle bags, bridle, hobbles, picket pins and McClellan saddle. I'll take you over to the supply store and Tommy will help you. Then we will have to get you settled in." The general led the way, with Clinton following. They walked into a small building, where a man was polishing a saddle. "Tommy, this is First Lieutenant Clinton McKay, our new recruit. He needs to be outfitted."

Tommy set the saddle aside. "Yes, General."

The general left and Tommy began piling items into Clinton's hands, by the time he was finished, Clinton's knees were about to buckle.

How am I going to carry all of this? Clinton thought and wondered where he was supposed to put everything. He looked at Tommy with pleading eyes.

"Lieutenant, I will give you a hand," Tommy said. "We might still have to make two trips to get everything."

"Much obliged, Tommy."

Clinton and Tommy each had their arms full. They walked across the parade ground towards the barracks. "Here we go, Lieutenant. This is your home for the time being so try and make yourself comfortable. I will go up the stairs with you, you will need to find a spare bunk bed."

"Thank you, Tommy."

Clinton and Tommy entered the cavalry barracks and walked up the squeaky stairwell. Clinton noticed the mess hall was downstairs as well as the laundry room. The dormitory was upstairs, decked out with wooden single slat beds in two rows on each side; they were so tiny that one move to the left or right at night would see the occupant topple onto the wooden floorboards.

Clinton walked through the centre of the hall, trying to find a spare bed; there were name cards on top of the bright blue open cupboards, where bridles and uniforms hung. Clinton eventually found a spare bed right at the end. There was a flimsy white bedroll used as a mattress, a standard wool blanket and a pillow. *Home sweet home for me*, Clinton thought as Tommy threw the items he was carrying on the bed. Clinton looked around the room, it seemed quite airy and bright with blue window sills and green bed heads. He was happy to be here.

Two days later, Clinton had his first assignment with the cavalry division: escort immigrants and stagecoaches through the Bozeman Trail with his trusty new steed, Ranger.

"Now, Ranger, if you look after me I will look after you. I need your help on this one. I'm a bit green to the open plains." Ranger neighed in what Clinton thought was understanding. Clinton checked the saddle and girth to make sure it was tight enough. They were out in the parade grounds with the rest of the seventy-eight soldiers, waiting for the call to mount. "Hey, Jacob, what's it like fighting Indians?" Jacob was chewing tobacco beside his jet black horse.

"It's very different to fighting in the Civil War. The Indians are very shifty. One minute they're in front of you and the next they're behind you. They can see us but we can never see them. I get quite nervous being out here — you never know if someone's going to fire an arrow into you. Clinton, whatever happens, remember to leave a bullet for yourself when fighting Injuns."

Clinton raised an eyebrow. "Why is that?"

"Well, let's just say if they capture you, you don't want to be alive. This is completely different to fighting in the Civil War, you have to think differently. You may not see any Injuns, but I can assure you that they can see you. A lot of the times they send decoy parties, expecting you to chase them, and once you do, you fall into their trap and become outnumbered. You're a bit of a greenhorn when it comes to Injuns, aren't you?"

"Yeah, got that right. I don't know anything about them, but I'm no greenhorn when it comes to fighting and surviving."

The bugle call sounded to mount. "Okay, Ranger, this is it." Clinton mounted his horse and he and the other cavalry members proceeded with the immigrants, stage-coaches and supply wagons. There was so much noise: horses neighing, bullocks and cows mooing, the clink of riding gear, people talking — not to mention the dust.

"Hey, Jacob, I'm pretty sure the Indians know we're coming," Clinton said.

"Well, we certainly can't hide from them. If we weren't here to protect these people, they would be fair game. Not long ago, a family of six German immigrants were travelling alone and the Sioux killed them all, except a young girl who was never found. Originally, they were meant to travel with another four groups of travellers but their girl was sick at that time so they couldn't go."

"That is a terrible tragedy for the poor family," remarked Clinton.

When Clinton turned back, he saw the mirage of wagon trains, animals and the immigrants — they all had purpose and courage. The prairie was endless, but Clinton enjoyed the freedom and fresh air. He liked the element of danger — it got his blood pumping. He continued to survey the horizon as they travelled, just in case the Indians showed themselves. He was fascinated by them, wondering who they were and what made them such fierce enemies.

"Do you have a sweetheart back home?" Jacob asked.

"Can't say that I do, not for a very long while. I was in the Civil War for years, and when that was over I went back home with my sister and nieces. Looking back, I don't think I've really missed a woman's company that much. You just learn to live without it. It makes you much stronger, and more independent, not having a woman around."

"I have a woman, her name's Mary. We met in New York, which is where I'm from, but I thought I'd try my luck in the west. Someone told me to join the army because at least I'd be employed, even though it's a hard life. So that's what I did, and Mary said she'll come be with me eventually, but I'm still waiting. I've sent letters but had no replies, and now I'm getting worried."

"I'm sure there is a good explanation, just keep writing until you get an answer. You never know, she could be planning to get out here this very moment."

"I've got my doubts, Clinton." Jacob sighed. "Maybe she's changed her mind."

"Don't give up just yet, find out what's happening. I'm sure she's been held up for some reason or another."

"Thanks, Clinton. You've given me incentive to send another letter, and I'll contact her ma and pa and see if they can tell me where she is."

They continued to chat while they made their way along the trail, making sure to keep an eye out for any Indians, but they didn't spot one. They made it through the trail safely, where they parted ways with the grateful immigrants and other travellers. The immigrants were on their own now, making their way to California or wherever their heart desired. The cavalry had done their job escorting them through the most dangerous territory. It was time for them to turn back, rest their horses and make camp after a long journey. It was late afternoon. The sun was still shining and touched the prairie grass, making it glow.

The cavalry was in double file, horses walking with their heads down low, stretching their necks on their loose reins. Suddenly, the air filled with shooting arrows. The horses started rearing up, with the riders holding on to them for dear life. The arrows came thick and fast. "Retreat! Retreat!" shouted Captain Larsen, who was commanding the troops.

They galloped back where they came from and found a large cluster of trees to give them cover. As the troops followed Captain Larsen into the trees, he commanded, "Dismount. Dismount. Find cover. Find cover. Every fourth trooper is to become a horse holder. Take the horses back into the woods. Keep your heads down. Keep your heads down."

Clinton jumped off Ranger and surrendered him to one of the horse holders. Jacob was right with Clinton, and they lay flat on their bellies with the other troops, hoping to find cover behind any felled logs, small bushes, or clumps of dirt. Some of the troops grabbed their sabres and started to dig furiously into the ground to gain some sort of cover.

Clinton noticed an Indian with a single feather in his hair on a pinto pony, running his horse along the hill in full view of the soldiers. The Indian's face was painted yellow with red hail spots on one side of his arm and a thunder bolt down his other arm.

Suddenly, a shrilling noise pierced the air.

"What is that noise, Jacob?" whispered Clinton.

"Bone whistles," Jacob said, whispering as well. "The Injuns breathe into them to create that shrill noise, which is meant to unnerve the enemy."

"Well, it's doing a good job."

"Keep your nerve, Clinton. Keep your nerve."

The same Indian warrior whipped his fiery pinto pony, charging towards the hiding cavalry.

"FIRE!" Captain Larsen ordered.

Soldiers fired at the Indian but missed. The Indian urged his horse on, getting closer and closer. He was within two metres of the soldiers' line when he turned back as quickly as he came. The volleys of gunfire kept on coming and was deafening. The Indian's horse reared up before collapsing, riddled with bullets. The Indian sprung to his feet and bolted in a zigzag fashion towards the safety of his tribesman, who were waiting patiently to strike. One bullet smashed through his skull, leaving him lifeless on the ground.

"What was the point of doing that, Jacob?" Clinton asked, taking a deep breath after the firing had ceased.

"He wanted to show his bravery — it was kind of like a suicide mission."

"But what a waste of a life. If he'd stayed back he would still be alive."

"Stop asking me questions. This is not the time or place for it. Concentrate on what you're doing. They're all still out there."

Suddenly, arrows flew from all directions. Hundreds of warriors were circling and charging at the soldiers, trying to decimate them. The Indians knew they had strength in numbers. The soldiers started to fire wildly, panicking.

Clinton looked down to reload his gun. White hot pain sliced through his right arm. "Argh! Argh! I've been hit!" He glanced at his arm. An arrow was stuck in it, blood gushing out around it.

"Clinton, hang on. Keep your head down." Jacob crawled on his stomach to get to Clinton's other side. "The arrow's gone halfway through your arm. We need to get it out."

"I don't want to die like this." Clinton clenched his teeth against the throbbing pain. They were still at the front of the firing line with bullets and arrows flying past them. Jacob could only think of one thing to do to get his friend to safety.

"When I count to three, I'm going to drag you to the horse holders. Doctor Porter should be there somewhere. We're lucky he decided to come on this journey. Are you ready, Clinton?" Clinton nodded. "One. Two. Three. Go."

With all of Jacob's might, he stood up and dragged

Clinton towards the back line, leaving a trail of blood behind them. Arrows were still flying everywhere and spasmodic gun shots fired. With God's mercy, they made it safely to where the horse holders were.

"Where's the doc?" Jacob asked frantically to another injured soldier who was groaning, holding an arrow protruding from his stomach. The soldier pointed to the right and there was a whole line of injured soldiers, some moaning in pain, some silent — gone to the eternal sky.

Doctor Porter was wrapping a bandage around a soldier's arm when he saw Jacob with Clinton and rushed over. "Lie still, trooper. I'll need to break the arrow and then pull it through. You'll need to hold him down," Doctor Porter told Jacob. "This is going to hurt."

Jacob retrieved a stick from the ground and put it in Clinton's mouth. "Bite down on this."

Doctor Porter broke the arrow in half and started to pull it through. Clinton clenched his jaw on the stick and the world spun as pain exploded in his arm. Blackness seeped into his vision.

"He is out cold, Doc," Jacob said. "What are we going to do? Is he going to die?"

"I'm going to put a tourniquet around his arm to staunch the bleeding. I need to operate quickly and sew the wound. It looks like it nicked an artery."

Gunfire exploded in the background. Jacob gulped and hoped the Indians weren't gaining any further ground; otherwise, arrows might start flying over here. "Isn't it risky to operate out here?"

"I have no other choice. He'll bleed out by the time we return to camp. I need you to keep holding him down as he may wake up and any sudden jolt could cause heavy bleeding. Alright here goes."

Doctor Porter made an incision in the arm to examine the damaged artery. The blood was flowing freely. He yelled out, "I need someone. Quickly! One of you horse holders, come now!" A young boy, not more than eighteen approached. "Come on, boy. I need you to put your fingers on this ruptured artery while I sew. It will stop the bleeding." The boy hesitated, he looked quite pale. "Come on, boy. This man is in trouble."

The boy placed his fingers in the wound and the bleeding eased. Doctor Porter sewed as quickly as possible. Clinton started to groan.

"Doc, I think he's waking up," Jacob said.

"I'm nearly done. Hold him steady."

The doctor managed to finish closing the wound before Clinton's eyes flew open, darting around wildly. "Where am I?"

"Everything is alright, soldier," the doctor assured him. "The arrow nicked an artery, but I've repaired it. You've lost a lot of blood, but you'll be fine. Now just lie still."

The Indian battle raged on, with more soldiers falling to the Indians' arrows. The Indians retreated once night fall began its decent. Captain Larsen approached Doctor Porter, who was tending to the wounded. "Doctor Porter, what is the situation with the wounded?"

"There are fifteen with superficial wounds, another thirty with middle stage wounds and ten seriously wounded who should not be moved for at least another couple of days. Not to mention the troops who didn't make it."

"We cannot stay here for another couple of days. We are sitting ducks. Are you sure we can't move the wounded?" asked Captain Larsen.

"I am against all wounded being moved. Any sudden jolt in movement could re-open their wounds."

Captain Larsen was silent a moment, pondering his decision. "We cannot stay here. The Indians will come back for us at daybreak. Red Cloud's warriors are fierce and once they know we're here, they'll keep coming until we are no more."

"But, Captain, what are you going to do? You cannot leave the wounded. The Sioux will scalp them alive. There must be another way."

"I really don't know what to do," said Captain Larsen. He rubbed his chin, deep in thought. "We need to move out at midnight and return to the fort under the cover of darkness, that is the only way. We'll have to leave the wounded here with an attachment of cavalry. Will you stay behind and look after the wounded?"

"I don't think I have much choice in the matter."

"Once they are fit to travel, you can return to the fort."

"That depends if we make it through alive, Captain. I feel really unsure about this."

"I have to make a decision and it's just not practical to keep every man here."

As midnight approached, the captain made arrangements for most of the cavalries' departure. Jacob approached Clinton, who was still lying on the ground, with a blood-stained bandage around his arm. "How are you feeling?"

"Like someone opened me up and stitched me back up in a hurry. My arm feels like lead."

"You are very lucky to be alive, Clinton."

"I know. I'm very grateful to the doc, yourself and the young boy for saving me." Clinton noticed the soldiers getting organised for their departure. "What's going on? There seems to be a lot of commotion."

"Most of the cavalry are moving out at midnight. Captain Larsen is leaving some men behind to protect and look after the wounded until they're fit to travel. You and the other injured soldiers cannot move for the next couple of days. I volunteered to stay behind."

"Gee, Jacob, that's mighty of you to do, but don't feel you have to stay on my behalf."

"Well, we have struck up a nice friendship, so it's my duty to look after you."

"I feel bad that I am holding everyone up."

"There are many others also badly wounded that cannot be moved so don't feel guilty — you didn't ask to get hit with an arrow. The soldiers that are staying behind are going to bury the bodies of the dead at dawn. You better get some sleep now."

Jacob left Clinton and gathered with the other soldiers who were staying behind, still seeking cover behind the trees. They were so exhausted no one had the energy to speak. The night sky cleared and a beautiful full moon appeared, lighting up the way for the soldiers who were readying to depart tonight.

As the clock struck midnight, three quarters of the cavalry were marching out, the rest staying behind to take care of the wounded. Captain Larsen approached Doctor Porter, who was watching over the wounded. "Doctor, all the preparations have been made. There is sufficient ammunition and food, but water needs to be sourced. The soldiers are going to dig in a bit further and make breastworks in case of attack."

"Very well, but where are we going to find water?"

"I have spoken to Captain Jones. He knows there is a small river behind us, not too far at all. He will send a water party before dawn so they can get back before the Indians attack — *if* they decide to attack, that is."

"Do you think we will make it?" asked Doctor Porter.

"I don't see why not. Everything is a gamble on the plains. No one knows what will happen. Good Luck, Doctor Porter. I will see you back at the fort."

"Safe travels, sir." The long line of soldiers left, riding their horses in single file.

The soldiers left behind watched their comrades depart, feeling very unsettled. There was no safety in numbers now. The soldiers laid down on the dirt, trying to get sleep and took turns keeping watch. No one could sleep though, despite their exhausted bodies wanting to. Although the night dragged on, it gave them peace as they knew the Indians didn't usually fight at night.

Once dawn approached though, they knew it would be a different story.

10

The Hiding

In the early hours of the morning, when the sun was just beginning to rise, the water party was safely back with enough water to last them through the day. Everything was quiet — too quiet. Every little sound from a bush rustling in the wind to a bird calling made the soldiers jump, and had them searching the plains for a glimpse of the Indians.

Without warning, an arrow hit a soldier between the eyes, killing him instantly. More arrows followed, but there were not as many flying through the air as there had been yesterday.

Doctor Porter was attending to the wounded when Captain Jones approached him. "What do you think is going on here, Captain Jones?" asked Doctor Porter.

"The arrow fire is not very heavy. You would think they would throw everything at us. They may just be trying to spook us or let us waste our ammunition so when they do finally charge us, there'll be less bullets flying around. It seems really odd, but I'm not complaining if they don't want to fight. Expect the unexpected, that's what I've learned from being out on the plains. Let's just keep our heads down," Captain Jones replied, fiddling with the buttons on his cavalry jacket, a sign of nervousness.

The soldiers were still very tense and did not move unless they needed to tend to the wounded — no one spoke, just kept their heads down. After the brief skirmish with the Indians, there was no more firepower or arrows. The morning went slowly for the soldiers; they hid behind the trees, dazed, not knowing what to do. Seeing this, Captain Jones gave them duties to do that afternoon, such as attending to the wounded, finishing the digging of makeshift trenches, keeping the camp tidy and counting food stocks as they were running low. They would also need to ration water supplies until morning. The soldiers started to relax and the wounded breathed more easily, hoping it wouldn't be too long before they were fit to travel and to get out of this precarious position.

The next day, the soldiers walked around the vicinity to stretch their legs, having been cooped up too long. They were still cautious and didn't travel very far. The wounded were improving. The Indians had vanished into thin air. The soldiers continued their duties and were regaining their confidence, beginning to chat with one another.

That afternoon, Doctor Porter checked on his patients. They were all recovering well. He wanted to move the wounded out as soon as possible. His instinct told him the Indians would be back. It was just a matter of when. He looked at Clinton, who was still lying on the ground, and asked, "How are you feeling today? I'm going to change your dressing and look at your wound."

"I'm feeling okay, thanks, Doc. I'm getting better each day, but still feel as though someone chopped my arm off."

Doctor Porter examined Clinton's arm. "Your wound looks as if it's healing nicely — there are no signs of infection, which is good."

Clinton glanced around at the other wounded men. "How is everyone else, Doc?"

"They are improving each day as well, but you have made significant improvement, considering your wound. You must be made of tough stuff."

"Fighting in the Civil War makes you pretty tough, but maybe it's the excellent medical care you've given me."

"Saving lives is all part of my job," Doctor Porter said. He finished making his rounds before finding Captain Jones. He was leaning against a tree trunk, looking towards the horizon. "Excuse me, Captain Jones."

Captain Jones turned around. "Yes, Doctor Porter. What can I do for you?"

"I wanted to give you a report on the wounded."

"What's the report," said Captain Jones, starting to fiddle with the buttons on his cavalry jacket again.

"The worst of the wounded are healing well and should be able to travel. There is no sign of infection in anyone's wounds. I have run out of bandages and other medical supplies. There is not much I can do here now. When can we go?" Doctor Porter asked eagerly.

"If they are ready as you say, we will move out tomorrow

night. I will give the wounded one more day of rest. The Indians seem to have forgotten about us."

The next morning couldn't come quicker for Doctor Porter; he was so eager to depart that he started whistling, which was unusual for him. He was a quiet man who didn't like fuss. The news of their intended departure spread like wildfire and the soldiers were in a jovial mood.

Everyone was excited about leaving. Captain Jones was making plans for the departure and gave his men individual instructions — everyone was going to contribute. Clinton was sitting propped up against a fallen log. Jacob was rationing water for the wounded, giving them all a drink out of an army flask. He came to Clinton, offering water.

Clinton took a sip and then said, "Thank you so much, Jacob, for sticking by me. I owe you one."

"That's alright, Clinton. It hasn't been as bad as I thought it would be with the Indians. I thought it was going to be one hard battle to survive their onslaught. Maybe they took pity on us." He shrugged.

"I don't know. Something is strange about that, but I'm not complaining. I thought if they broke through to our defences that I'd be as good as dead, considering I can't defend myself right now," said Clinton, relieved.

"So, Clinton, everything is being worked out for our departure at midnight," said Jacob.

"I'm looking forward to it, but I'm worried about the ride back. I can only use one arm," Clinton said, concerned.

"Ranger is pretty steady. I think he'll look after you."

"I know. I love my horse. We have a real bond. He understands me."

"You are lucky to have fallen in love that quickly, even if it is with a horse."

The day went by very quickly for the men. By the time it was eleven that night, everything was done: the horses were saddled and the soldiers were ready. An hour before the scheduled departure, Captain Jones instructed, "All men, we need to help the wounded on their horses."

Jacob went to find Ranger, who was tied up to a makeshift post. He led Ranger to Clinton who was standing, waiting to be helped.

"I'll give you a hand, Clinton," said Jacob, bringing Ranger who neighed when he saw his owner.

"I might need more than a hand. I'm not sure I have the strength to lift myself up."

"I'll give you a leg up. Put your left arm on top of the saddle for balance. We will go slowly. Ready?"

"Yes, but be careful."

"Here goes."

Clinton braced himself and before he knew it, he was in the saddle.

Once everyone was mounted, they began their journey back to the fort. The march was slow through the darkness, with the soldiers relying on their horses to get them through enemy territory. They rested every two hours for twenty minutes, feeling safe under the cover of darkness.

Hours passed quickly and the moonlight gradually dispersed as the sun rose and the birds began singing.

"How are you travelling, Clinton?" asked Jacob, riding beside him.

Looking down, Clinton noticed blood seeping from the bandage on his arm. "Not good, Jacob. I'm bleeding."

"I'll get the doc." Jacob cantered his horse to the front where Doctor Porter was riding beside Captain Jones. "Doctor Porter, Clinton's bleeding."

The cavalry halted while Doctor Porter followed Jacob back to Clinton, who dismounted his horse with Jacob's help.

"Let's have a look," Doctor Porter said, dismounting his own horse. He unravelled the bandage and noticed a few of the stiches were broken. "I need to stich your arm back up. We have to do it here, and it will hurt."

Clinton laid on the ground while Doctor Porter gave him the last swig of whiskey from his flask.

"Clinton, you will have to be as quiet as you can. Remember, we are still in hostile territory. Here's a stick to bite down on." Doctor Porter put a thick piece of wood in Clinton's mouth.

Clinton bit down as the needle pierced his skin, hoping it would be over soon.

"All done, Clinton," Doctor Porter said a short time later. "Be very careful when mounting that horse — no sudden movements."

Jacob and Doctor Porter helped Clinton get back on Ranger before returning to their own horses. The march began again, and as they progressed through enemy territory, they spotted immigrants passing through — five wagons with women and children.

"Jacob, why are they endangering their lives like that?" Clinton asked.

"I suppose they don't understand the dangers this country brings. They are bravely taking a chance, though I know for sure they won't get to their destination. Those poor kids."

"Can we stop them?"

"You can try. I don't know if they'll listen."

"I have to try." Clinton broke out of formation and approached the man in the wagon. "Excuse me, sir. I'm First Lieutenant Clinton McKay. This is a very dangerous trail. The Sioux Indians patrol this area and will attack your group. Our outfit is heading back to Fort Laramie, you should follow us back. I doubt the Sioux will let you through, and I'm sure you don't want to lose your life."

"I know it's dangerous, but we have to take a chance. We want to start a new life and that passion overrides the dangers. But as we were passing through we saw some bodies," the man said.

"What do you mean, sir? What bodies were there?"

"They were in uniform, not far from the trail."

"How many?"

"I don't know, maybe twenty to thirty. Maybe fifty." Clinton looked into the distance with a glazed look, thinking about what the man had just said. *It can't be*, Clinton thought. *The man must be mistaken.* "Are you sure they were in uniform?"

"Yes, Lieutenant. I know what I saw."

Clinton took a deep breath and told the man, "Well, it's up to you if you want to turn back or face the Sioux."

"We cannot turn back. Our whole future depends on us getting to California, and we cannot waste any time. We need to get there as quickly as possible."

"Suit yourself, but I wouldn't recommend it."

Clinton left the wagon train and approached Captain Jones. "Captain, I was over by the wagon train and an immigrant reported bodies not too far from where we are — and they are in uniform, Captain."

"What are you saying? That they are part of our division?"

"I don't know for sure, but it seems that way. The immigrant said roughly twenty to thirty, maybe even fifty, bodies."

"Oh dear God, it just cannot be." Captain Jones was in shock.

With much hesitation, they continued along the trail with their entire focus on their environment, looking for signs that would lead them to the bodies that were presumably cavalry. They kept in close formation and alert to the sounds around them, even the rustle of the prairie grass and the wind whistling past their faces. They passed over a high knoll that led them to a flat open prairie land and to their dismay, they saw what they were dreading.

"Cavalry, apart from the wounded, dismount. We need to check these bodies to see who they are, and bury them if possible."

Clinton rode Ranger through the bodies and felt sad and angry that this happened. They all had arrows sticking out of them, and some were scalped, with items of clothing removed.

"Men, I have counted thirty-five bodies from our outfit," Captain Jones said after he had finished moving through the dead bodies. "We need to stay and bury them. Use anything you have that can scrape the earth, such as sabres or tin cups," Captain Jones said, voice tight with emotion.

No sooner had the captain finished talking, Clinton noticed a group of men on horseback on the horizon. "Look, Captain! Over there," Clinton yelled.

"What is it?" Captain Jones looked through his field glasses and sighed with relief, recognising twenty cavalrymen with wagons approaching. "Men, it is the cavalry." He signalled them down.

The cavalry and wagons approached quickly on seeing their comrades. Lieutenant Slade, leading the party, trotted his horse directly to the captain and saluted.

"Captain Jones, we are glad to see you once again, and alive for that matter," said Lieutenant Slade.

"Lieutenant, do you know what happened here?" Captain Jones asked.

"The Sioux's war parties, that's what happened. Captain Larsen reported a Sioux attack. They had them pinned down for about two hours, most of them made it back to the fort. The war party wasn't a huge one and left after a while. Captain Larsen reported what happened with you all, but we were doubtful you would make it back. We have come to collect the bodies to bury them at the fort — it's too risky to bury them here."

Everyone, aside from the wounded, helped load the bodies onto the wagons and headed back to Fort Laramie. They finally made it back and the soldiers wanted to kiss the ground in appreciation of their safe return. There was no rest for them; they attended to their horses first — feeding, watering and grooming them, before even thinking about themselves. The wounded that could help did, but the rest were ordered to their quarters or to the hospital where Doctor Porter kept an eye on them. Clinton was instructed to see Doctor Porter before he returned to his quarters. His arm was going to be put in a sling to stabilise it so the stiches didn't break again.

That afternoon, the soldiers started burying bodies and writing names on anything they could find to mark the graves.

Two days had passed since the soldiers had returned home. Clinton was recovering well. He was wandering around the fort, still with his arm in a sling, tired of being cooped up. He wanted to check on Ranger in the stables. As he was heading in that direction, out of the corner of his eye he saw a horse and rider galloping towards him, going at breakneck speed. Suddenly, Clinton was covered in dust.

"Hello," said the horse's rider, a beautiful woman with blonde curls and sea green eyes that danced with excitement.

Clinton spluttered from the dust and eventually found his voice. "Do you always shower people with a dust storm?" Clinton remarked, coughing the dust from his lungs.

"I do it when I see fit."

"What is that meant to mean? You like covering lieutenants in dust?"

"Only the ones who look good in uniform."

"Miss, are you trying to flatter me?"

"What if I am? There's no harm done."

Clinton smirked. "I have never heard a woman be so forthcoming."

"Well, Lieutenant, maybe you haven't met a real woman before," the woman said with a smile.

Clinton chuckled. "Perhaps that's true — real women are hard to come by, especially in these parts. Where are you from?"

"Texas."

"I should have known by your southern drawl. I haven't heard a Texas accent for a while, apart from fighting against them in the war." The woman flinched. "Sorry, I didn't mean to upset you."

"I just want to forget the horrid war. My father brought my mother and me here to start afresh, but everyone keeps reminding me about the war, probably because we were on the losing side."

"The war is over now. All American people are equal. You know how people can talk," reassured Clinton.

"Yes, I do, Lieutenant, but we have forgotten the most important part of getting to know each other, our names."

"My name is Clinton McKay. First Lieutenant Clinton McKay."

"I am Nancy Colby." She reached for his hand in good will.

"Pleased to meet you, Miss Colby."

"Please just call me Nancy."

"As you wish, Nancy. You said you are here with your mother and father. Any other siblings?" Clinton asked.

"No. I am an only child. My family lives in the officers' quarters. My father is General Colby."

"Of course. I should have realised that when you mentioned your surname."

"Details, Lieutenant. You have to be much more attentive than that."

"My apologies. Lovely horse you are riding, Nancy." Clinton stroked the horse.

"This is my Kentucky thoroughbred mare, Flash. Eventually I will breed her. She has a mind of her own and is quite feisty and uncontrollable, especially when she smells wild animals," Nancy said proudly.

"I bet you two are a match made in heaven." Clinton started chuckling.

"Are you implying I may be uncontrollable?"

"The thought did cross my mind." Clinton chuckled again.

"Well, Lieutenant, we should go for a ride some time. What type of horse do you ride? I will race you whenever you feel up to the challenge."

"My horse is a Clydesdale cross named Ranger, and we are not up to racing a Kentucky thoroughbred."

"I can always give you a head start, but I have every intention of beating you."

"Is that so, Nancy?"

"Yes, and I am sure I will see you soon. I will find you, don't worry about that. I have enjoyed your company so far."

Before Clinton could respond, Nancy galloped away. All Clinton could see was her blonde hair blowing in the wind, her tight knit curls bouncing up and down. He liked her, but as she was an officer's daughter, courting her was too risky to even attempt.

Clinton continued his walk to the stables. There was a lot of activity: horses being groomed, stalls being mucked out, horses being saddled to be exercised. Clinton greeted the soldiers as he made his way to Ranger, who had his head in his feed bin. The minute Ranger saw Clinton approaching, he rushed to the front of his stall.

"Hi, boy," Clinton said. "How do you feel about racing a Kentucky thoroughbred?"

Ranger neighed.

"Don't worry, boy, we'll find a short cut somehow. No Clydesdale cross can beat a thoroughbred, but if we can't win the race, maybe we can win the girl. But don't lose any sleep over it, boy. I don't think we should race her anyway. She just wants to show off, and of course she's going to win on a Kentucky thoroughbred. Not to worry. We don't need to prove ourselves to anyone. We're a team now, Ranger."

Ranger neighed in approval.

II

Mamie

Nancy hadn't slept all night. She had been thinking about the man she'd met the other day. She was hopeful she would see Clinton this morning, though she needed to get ready first. She picked her favourite blue and white checked dress, which complemented her sea green eyes. She brushed her blonde hair about fifty times to make it shine before washing her face. She hurried down the stairwell and could smell something delicious cooking in the kitchen.

"Good morning, Mamie," Nancy said to the housemaid, who was busying herself at the stove. "I am starving." Nancy sat down at the table, waiting for her breakfast.

"Good morning, yourself. Hotcakes today. Your father's favourite." Mamie finished flipping the hotcakes in the hot fat and stacked a plate for Nancy. "There you are, child."

"Thank you, Mamie." Nancy gobbled down her breakfast, which nearly got stuck halfway down her throat.

"Nancy, slow down. I didn't cook your breakfast for you to choke," Mamie said.

"Sorry, Mamie. I am just so excited to start the day."

Mamie wiped her hands on her apron, expecting the rest of the family at any moment.

"Do you believe in love at first sight?" Nancy asked.

"That came out of the blue. Well, I don't know. I fell in love with a fellow slave called Jay on the plantation. We got to know each other first so it wasn't love at first sight. I believe it's a lot of hogwash," commented Mamie, while making some more batter for the hotcakes.

"Did you love Jay?" asked Nancy, interested.

"That was a long time ago and I don't know if I did love him or not. I was only young at the time, and I don't know what happened to him. He never said goodbye. He simply vanished and for him to just leave like that... well, I knew it wasn't real love."

"Why did he leave?"

"I don't know. He escaped off the plantation. That was a heartbreaking time for me. I thought my heart would never heal, but to my surprise it did, and I met someone else on the plantation, Al, and had two children, Ivana and Celeste, who are with me here at the fort. You haven't met them yet. They work in the laundry. We call it Suds Row."

"Where is your husband? I am sorry for all these questions, Mamie. I just want to know more about you."

"There were certain people who didn't like the idea of slavery being illegal, they wanted to take matters into their own hands. We left the plantation after the Civil War, as we were free and Al said this was our chance, but you know a lot of people didn't leave the plantation as they had nowhere to go, so they stayed. Al was always hopeful that we would find a better life somehow. We stayed in an empty shack that was abandoned during the war. It was only temporary until we found some place else.

"Once the war was over, people acted very strange, even though we were free. We were still just slaves to a lot of them. Some people taunted us. They didn't want us there. A group of men took my husband and I never saw him again... I presume they hanged him. I was screaming in hysterics. There was nothing I could do. Al knew he wouldn't live, I saw it in his eyes — the pure terror. Oh, my poor Al. I cannot speak anymore. It was the worst night of my life. I remember it so vividly. My children still have nightmares about it." Mamie's eyes filled with tears that streaked down her cheeks; she wiped them with the corner of her apron.

"Oh, Mamie, I am so sorry. I didn't know. Please forgive me. I didn't mean to upset you."

"It's alright, child. It is very painful to talk about it as it wasn't that long ago."

"You certainly have had a lot of heartbreak in your life."

"Yes, I have. Let's talk about something else, so what were you saying about love?"

"Oh, Mamie, I think I am in love and I do believe it's love at first sight."

"So, who is the lucky man?"

"First Lieutenant Clinton McKay. He's the man I want to marry."

"Steady on, child, you just met him."

"He is charming and handsome and has that special twinkle in his eye."

"Well, child, you have to be careful of those men who have that special twinkle in their eye."

They both burst into laughter.

"Don't forget, your father is the general. It may be a bit awkward if you were courting a lieutenant. Your father might have a say in that."

"Leave Father to me. He can't control whom I see."

They heard footsteps coming down the squeaky stairwell and fell quiet. A moment later, General Colby walked in with his wife, Marie, and both sat down at the table.

"Good Morning, ladies," said General Colby. "Breakfast smells great, Mamie. I am starving and need something hearty. A lot of training and drilling today, getting the new recruits ready for a campaign."

Mamie and Nancy looked at each other and smiled while Mamie poured the fresh batter into the hot pan.

"Nancy, you are up early today," General Colby remarked.

"Yes, Father, there is always something to do. You just can't waste a moment."

"I like your attitude. You should train these new recruits and hopefully your attitude will rub off on them. Marie, you have been awfully quiet this morning. Is everything alright?"

"Yes, Charles. Sometimes it's hard to get a word in when you're rambling."

"Oh, please. I don't ramble. You just think that I do."

Marie rolled her eyes. "Now, Nancy, your mother is going to organise a social soon and she will need your help."

"Yes, Mother, I will help you. When are we going to hold the social?"

"In a couple of weeks. It will be good for the Fort to break up the boredom and get to know everyone," informed Marie.

"Well, that is settled then. Nancy, you will help your mother — and make sure the piano is tuned. Your mother and yourself can play some tunes so people can dance."

"Charles, we can organise it. You concentrate on your duties, not on ours," Marie said assertively.

Mamie placed hotcakes in front of General Colby and Marie.

"Alright, dear, but you will also need to organise food and drink, and if there is going to be dancing, we will need extra females to dance with."

"Charles! I am not going to tell you again. We are capable of arranging this."

"Alright, I won't say another word but..."

"Charles!"

"Only kidding, just stirring the pot."

"I think it is about time you went on duty."

"Not before I finish my hotcakes."

"May I be excused?" Nancy pushed to her feet. "I am going for an early morning ride. I will see you soon, Mother, to start organising," said Nancy, ready to find Clinton.

"Very well, dear, just remember not to go outside the Fort's perimeter," said a concerned Marie.

Nancy approached the stables and entered Flash's stall. Flash had her ears pricked, tail swishing and was circling. She was ready to run, so Nancy quickly saddled her. No one else was around — all the troopers were still having breakfast. She mounted Flash and galloped from the stables, leaving dust in her wake. She rode all around the fort grounds, hoping for a glimpse of Clinton. She eventually spotted him walking towards the stables. Nancy couldn't resist and galloped straight to him.

"Good morning, Clinton, when can we race?"

Clinton stopped his walking and smiled at Nancy. "Good morning. I am still recovering from my wound and I am on light duties for the rest of the week."

"Well, that's not good, but now that you are on light duties, we can spend time together, sitting and talking."

"Not today. Captain Mason has asked me to do something."

"Surely you can find some time today."

"I will see how I go, but I cannot promise anything," Clinton said, scratching his head.

"Alright, Clinton, I will see you later."

"You are stubborn, aren't you? I never said I would officially see you today."

"I always get what I want." Nancy winked. "Bye, Clinton." Nancy continued riding.

Clinton was speechless. *She's a wild one*, he thought with

a shake of his head, before making his way to the stables to meet Captain Mason.

As soon as Clinton entered the stables, Captain Mason was right there, waiting. He was always punctual.

"Lieutenant McKay, I would like you to meet my niece Sarah."

Sarah inclined her head. "Pleasure to meet you, Lieutenant."

"And you ma'am." Sarah was seventeen years old. She had dark red hair that was tightly woven into two plaits that touched her elbows. Her hazel eyes matched the freckles on her face and she wore eyeglasses that were too big.

"Sarah is very excited to learn to fire a gun and also to ride a horse," Captain Mason explained. "She wants to get a taste of the American West — being a New Yorker, this is quite different for her. My family is visiting me — my sister, brother-in-law and Sarah. Please don't tell anyone you're teaching my niece about guns and riding horses. My sister is very proper and would have a fit if she knew what her daughter was up to."

"You have my word, Captain. It will keep me occupied while I recover."

"Sarah, I will leave you with Lieutenant McKay for a couple of hours. Be good." Captain Mason left to attend to his duties.

Sarah smiled at Clinton. "Thank you for offering your services, Lieutenant McKay."

"Call me Clinton, and I'm happy to help. I think we'll

start with how to handle a gun safely, and then we'll do some target practice. Can you stay here while I go to the ammunition store to get what I need?"

Sarah nodded. Clinton came back with a Carbine, ammunition and practice targets. "Miss Sarah, can you help me carry these things." Sarah came running to catch the practice targets, which were about to fall on the ground. "We will go over to the middle of the parade ground. There is no one there at the moment."

Sarah followed Clinton, her walking so clumsy she nearly dropped the practice targets. They stopped in the middle of the parade ground.

"Clinton, have you ever killed anyone?" Sarah asked while Clinton set everything up.

"Yes. If I could have avoided it, I would have, but then I wouldn't be standing here."

Clinton finished setting up the targets and held the gun. "Miss Sarah, watch what I do. Pay attention to how I hold the gun. There is no ammunition in the gun yet. Firstly, hold the gun in the middle of the barrel, raise it up in line with your elbow. Set your sights on your target and then squeeze the trigger with your right hand. Here, you try." Clinton gave Sarah the gun and she practised pretending to fire.

"That is good, Miss Sarah, now to the serious stuff. I am going to place ammunition in the gun. I want you to fire at the targets I've set up." Clinton took the gun back and loaded it. He fired at a target, hitting the bullseye. He handed the gun to Sarah. "Your turn."

Clinton made sure she was holding the gun properly and instructed her not to point at anything but the targets. Sarah pulled the trigger and the aftershock blasted her backwards, knocking her to the ground. Clinton offered his hand, helping her back to her feet. "I can't believe I did that. Let me try again."

"This time, ease the trigger slowly," instructed Clinton.

Sarah slowly pulled the trigger. The gun jerked and the shot fired into the sky. A meadowlark dropped to the ground. Sarah pressed a hand to her mouth. "Oh my, Clinton, what have I done?"

Clinton took the gun away from her. "Maybe we should go to the stables."

"Can I ride today?"

"No, not today. I am going to teach you how to put a saddle and bridle on a horse first. Let's head back."

Clinton led the way with Sarah following. They dropped the gear at the ammunition store and headed to the stables. Two hours later, Clinton had had enough and let Sarah go for the day before heading to the officers' quarters where Nancy was living. He needed to see her; he felt as if Nancy had put a spell on him.

Clinton was approaching the porch of Nancy's residence when Nancy saw him from the window while quilting with her mother in the dining area. Nancy raced out to the porch. "Clinton, you have come to see me. I told you I always get what I want."

"I think you are right, as I don't know why I'm here. You

must have a magical power over me," Clinton said as he was walking up the porch stairs.

"That's good to know." She smiled. "Please come in. I'll make you a cup of tea." They walked into the reading room where Marie was sitting. "Mother, this is First Lieutenant Clinton McKay. Lieutenant McKay, this is my mother Marie. We were doing some quilting, as you can see, but that's not all. We are organising a social for next Saturday and you have a special invitation."

Clinton inclined his head. "Pleasure to make your acquaintance ma'am."

Marie just smiled.

"Come and sit down, Clinton," Nancy said.

"I cannot stay long. I still have to commence my duties, as I had other things to attend to this morning. I will stay for a cup of tea though."

"What type of things?" Nancy asked impatiently.

"I cannot really say. It's army business."

"Army business. We know all about that, don't we, Mama?"

"Yes, we certainly do, especially me — being married to your father for twenty years makes you think there is no other life besides army life."

"My father gave me a job helping with the horses when needed, and doing other chores," Nancy explained before heading to the kitchen to organise tea.

"I've only just joined the cavalry and have already been christened with a Sioux arrow in the arm that almost killed me. Although I'm used to the ways of war, fighting the Indians is different," stated Clinton.

"Oh, how frightening to be at the hands of the Sioux. I cringe when I hear horror stories about the killings along the Bozeman Trail," said Marie.

"But, Mama, we see a lot of Indians around the fort when they come in to sign treaties and they look harmless enough," said Nancy, walking back in with a tray of tea things. "I find them quite fascinating. I love their feathered headdresses and the trinkets they wear." Nancy handed out the tea cups and sat beside Clinton.

"Oh, Nancy, how can you say that? How can you even look at them? I feel sorry for your father who has to deal with them all the time." Marie focused her attention on Clinton. "So, Lieutenant, how do you feel about them?"

"I honestly don't know. I really don't know much about them — only that they are good at firing arrows, but apart from that they seem to be a very strong and powerful people."

"Lieutenant, would you like to join us for dinner tonight? Our housekeeper, Mamie, is such a good cook," asked Marie, much to Nancy's joy.

"I appreciate the invitation, but don't think it is a good idea. It wouldn't sit well with the other soldiers. I don't want to get off side with them. I haven't been here that long." Nancy shot him a pleading look that begged him to change his mind. "What's that look for? You're expecting to get your own way again."

"Think about the invitation and if you change your

mind, you are more than welcome. Pleased to meet you, Lieutenant McKay," Marie said before going upstairs to give them some privacy to talk.

"Half past six is a good time," Nancy said.

Clinton chuckled. "No... I really shouldn't. Your father wouldn't want me at the table. Generals never eat with lieutenants. I'm afraid I will have to decline."

"Clinton, you can't say no. No one has ever said no to me. You don't want me to get upset."

"I'm sorry, Nancy, I can't. I have to go. Thank you for the tea." He pushed to his feet.

"Clinton, don't go."

"I will see you again soon." Clinton left, leaving Nancy standing with her hands on her hips, flabbergasted that someone had said no to her.

12

The Lesson

T he next bright and sunny morning, Clinton was waiting for Sarah in the stables, with Ranger beside him.
When she entered, she'd changed from the practical, femi-
nine girl he'd met yesterday into a tomboy. She was dressed
in fawn male trousers, a checked shirt with a dark brown
vest and a dowdy hat that sat above her tight bun.

"Good morning, Clinton. I am ready to learn how to ride."

"Hello, Miss Sarah. I didn't recognise you."

"Don't you love my new outfit?" She giggled. "I'm wearing these dowdy clothes so my mother and father don't see
me riding around the Fort. It really is me. See." She lifted
her hat off her head and as she did, Nancy approached the
stables and was shocked to see Clinton with another girl.
She hid behind a wooden beam so they wouldn't spot her,
her heart sinking.

"You can ride my horse Ranger today. He is all ready to
go, with his saddle and bridle," Clinton told Sarah. "He is
a gentleman. You will like him. Let's take him out."

Clinton led Ranger and Sarah to the parade ground,
where some of the soldiers were riding and exercising

horses. Clinton and Sarah headed to the outside of the circle to keep out of their way. Nancy was still watching from the stables, wondering why Clinton hadn't mentioned anything about this girl.

"Okay, let's begin," Clinton said. "Put your foot in the stirrup and pull yourself onto the saddle."

"That sounds easy enough." Sarah put her foot in the stirrup and tried to push herself up but failed. She tried again and failed. "Clinton, I'm having trouble."

"I'll give you a leg up. Place your left hand on the reins and your right hand on the saddle and I will push you up. One, two and three." Sarah was in the saddle.

"Now it's up to you, Miss Sarah. Hold the reins like this." Clinton mimicked holding reins. "That's perfect," he said when Sarah copied him. "Next give Ranger a little squeeze with your legs, and once he starts trotting sit deeply in the saddle."

Sarah squeezed Ranger's ribs with her legs. She tried to sit deep in the saddle as the horse began trotting, but her body was jerking left and right, completely out of sync with Ranger's movements.

"Sit deep. Keep your body still," Clinton called.

Gradually, her body synced with Ranger's, but her hands were flying up and down.

"Keep your hands down."

Sarah concentrated on keeping her hands lowered and grinned when they stopped jerking all over the place. After an hour, she started to get the hang of it. Clinton and Ranger were very patient with her. Ranger seemed to sense she was just starting out and was a well-behaved gentleman. Sarah thanked Clinton for the lesson and gave Ranger a huge pat before parting ways.

Nancy had watched the entire scene, maintaining her distance, and was not happy about what she'd seen. *Why was Clinton helping that girl ride? Was she trying to impress Clinton?* She retreated back towards her home with a sad frown on her face. She felt deflated that Clinton was keeping the company of another girl. She headed up to her bedroom and laid on her bed. Her stomach was in knots. After a half hour of lying down, she got her incentive back and thought to herself, *no one can get in the way of Clinton and me!*

Nancy left her room and headed down the porch steps. She entered the fort grounds, hoping to find Clinton. There he was, leading Ranger back to the stables. "Clinton, oh, Clinton."

Clinton turned around and said, "Oh, no. Here comes the terror."

"Clinton, I am personally inviting you to the social dance at my father's premises on Saturday at six thirty sharp."

"Nancy, you invited me yesterday."

"I did, but this is more of a personal invitation. I just wanted to see you, and if you behave yourself you may be able to dance with the belle of the ball."

"And who would that be?"

"Ha, ha, very funny. You know that would be me."

"I was just checking. You never know how many belles will be there, and I could have my pick of the selection."

"That is very funny, and I hope if you did have your selection that I would be at the top of your list."

"Of course, belle. I wouldn't want to dance with anyone else, but please tell me you don't have two left feet."

"You will find out when I step on your toes." They both chuckled. "Come on, let's have a dance lesson now so we can practise," Nancy said in an enthusiastic tone.

"I have a horse that I have to put back into his stall, and I can't take time out while I am in uniform. I have to get back to my duties," Clinton said, annoyed. He didn't like to dance and it wasn't an appropriate time; if he was caught, he would be in trouble.

"Just hitch Ranger on the post over there." Nancy pointed to the hitching posts adjacent to the stables. "Oh, come on, Clinton, just two minutes. Let's have some fun. No one is going to punish you. Have you forgotten I am the general's daughter?"

Clinton relented and hitched Ranger to the post, while Nancy waited with a big smile on her face. As Clinton made his way back to Nancy, he commented, "I don't know why I let you talk me into things."

"Let's go over to the side of the stables, towards the trees, so no one will see us."

When they arrived at their destination, Nancy initiated the dance. "Come and put one hand on my waist and your other in my hand. Don't be scared, no one is going to punish you for taking two minutes off."

"Very well, but remember my wound still hurts."

"I thought soldiers were meant to be tough."

Clinton rolled his eyes and took her hand, placing his other around her waist.

"Now, you need to count. One, two, three and four, two steps forward and two steps back, and turn. See you've got it now. Let's go faster," Nancy said bossily.

"Hold on, I can't keep up," Clinton said, frustrated, as they weaved between the trees.

"No, not that foot, you need to bring the other one forward. Come on, Clinton. You're not very co-ordinated, are you?"

"You're going too fast for me," Clinton argued.

"Come, let's try again and start with the right foot. Alright, go. Ouch! Clinton, you stepped on my foot. What are you doing? The lesson is over and, Clinton, you do not know how to dance," Nancy said with a chuckle.

"Maybe not, but you're not a good teacher. You go too fast and you don't explain things properly."

"What is there to explain? You just move your feet and count the beats."

"But there are no beats — there is no music."

"Then just hum your favourite tune and you'll find the beat. Clinton, you have to learn to dance. We still have time before the social. Come on, let's try again as you are not going to learn if you don't practise."

"I don't know. I might tread on your foot again."

"Stop being a baby. I promise I will be a better teacher."

"No, I'd rather not. I have to finish grooming Ranger and someone is calling me." Clinton was lying. "Can't you hear? I have to go. I will see you later."

"Clinton, come back. You can't get out of it that easily."

Clinton pretended not to hear her and unhitched Ranger, making his way to the stables. Nancy was frustrated the lesson didn't go how she'd thought it would, but that was not going to deter her.

Later that afternoon, Nancy spotted Clinton and Sarah together while she was talking to a family of immigrants who were making camp at Fort Laramie. Nancy stood behind their wagon, peering out from the side. She saw them laughing as they walked towards the stables. Sarah was playing with her hair, twirling it as she laughed — she was enjoying the attention. *What is Clinton doing? She is too young for him. She's only just finished school. What's he thinking? Obviously that girl is enjoying the attention, but hands off my man. I cannot let it go any further. I always get what I want!* She thought to herself.

Nancy excused herself from the conversation and walked to the stables, pretending to check on Flash. She entered the stables while Clinton was rationing feed for the horses. He turned around when he heard footsteps. "Hello, Nancy, what brings you here?"

"Hello, Clinton. I'm just checking on Flash." Nancy turned to Sarah while she was patting some of the horses. "I'm Nancy. And you are?"

"I am Sarah."

"What brings you to Fort Laramie?"

"I am visiting my uncle with my family. Clinton is making me feel welcome and showing me around."

"That is very kind of you, Clinton," Nancy said. "I bet he is looking after you real fine. So, what have you been up to? There is not much to show you around the fort, apart from horses, soldiers — maybe some immigrants — and perhaps some agency Indians."

"Well, Clinton has taught me a few things, I've learnt many things on my Wild West experience. My friends are going to be most jealous."

"Jealous? What do you mean jealous? What have you been doing?" demanded Nancy, worried.

Clinton tried to put her mind at ease. "It is alright, Nancy. You don't have to get antsy about it."

"But what have you been doing together? It sounds as though it's a big secret. You can tell me. I'm good at keeping secrets."

"I'm sure you are, but we cannot tell you. Word might get around the fort and then the people whom we are trying to keep this from will find out and Sarah will be in trouble as well as Captain Mason. Does that make sense?"

"What Clinton is trying to say is it is none of your business," said Sarah.

"What? None of my business? No one talks to me like that, missy. My father is the general here so don't get too comfortable."

Sarah poked her tongue at Nancy.

"Come on, that's enough, you two." Clinton stepped between them. "I'm sorry, Nancy. I cannot tell you at this moment as I gave Captain Mason my word. But it is nothing to worry about."

Nancy stormed out of the stables.

"What was all that about?" asked Sarah.

Clinton scratched his head. "I'm not sure, but I think she is upset that I didn't tell her about the time we are spending together."

"I think Nancy likes you. She wouldn't act that way if she didn't," said Sarah.

"You women can be hard to work out — very hot and cold. No wonder I haven't been involved with anyone for a while. Nancy is really feisty. She keeps me on my toes."

"We aren't all that bad," Sarah argued. "Maybe you just need to try harder to understand us. I will see you later." Sarah departed.

Clinton just stood there. "Women!"

13

The Dance

Nancy was upstairs in her bedroom, playing with her hair, making sure no strands were out of place. It was the night of the social dance being held in Nancy's family home. She wanted to look her best for Clinton. She decided a high bun with waves of blonde ringlets shaping her face would be the best style to choose. She wore one of her nicest dresses: a deep red burgundy dress with cream lace detail on the cuffs and hem, and a high neck collar. She coloured her lips deep red and added rouge to her cheeks. Butterflies fluttered in her stomach. *Clinton will be here soon.*

"Nancy, the guests are about to start arriving. We need to get organised," General Colby yelled from downstairs.

"Yes, Father, I am coming," said Nancy, shouting so her father could hear her. Feeling proud of how she looked, she slowly walked down the stairwell, careful not to trip on her flowing dress. As she came to the living area, her father and mother were attending to last minute details. They both turned around.

"Well, don't you look as pretty as a picture — you're

glowing," the general said. "Make sure you save a dance for your poor old father."

"Of course, Papa."

"You look really pretty, dear," her mother commented.

Nancy smiled.

The time was half past six. They were all waiting in the hallway for their guests. The general was pacing up and down and Marie was fiddling with the hem of her navy blue gown while Nancy was twirling her curls.

"I can hear people coming," General Colby said. He strode to the door to greet the first guests. "Welcome, Captain Larsen and the lovely Mrs Larsen. Please come in. You are the first of our guests. Everyone should be along shortly. I would like to introduce you to my other half, and better half — she does keep me in line. This is my precious wife, Marie, and my equally precious daughter Nancy."

Gradually, more guests arrived and the room was soon filled with people in their best outfits. Punch and food were served, satisfying everyone's appetite. Nancy kept looking at the door, hoping Clinton would arrive soon. Marie started playing the piano in the large supper room.

Nancy watched as couples began dancing, wishing Clinton was there. She noticed Lieutenant Mc Ably watching her; his gaze made her cheeks blush but she pretended not to notice. He made his way over to her, starting up a conversation. Nancy laughed and twirled her delicate ringlets, leaning towards him. She thought he was very charming.

"Would you like to dance, Miss Nancy?"

"Yes, Lieutenant."

"Please call me Stuart."

They joined the other couples on the floor, dancing to the piano music Marie was playing. *This is more pleasant than dancing with Clinton*, she thought to herself. Stuart's moves were graceful and in sync with her own and they danced until the music stopped for an interval.

"Let me acquire us some beverages," Stuart said and vanished, quickly returning with punch. He handed her a cup. "Here you are."

Stuart was flirting with Nancy shamelessly, which made Nancy flirtatious as well. She got carried away in the moment, liking the attention.

"Would you like a walk outside, Miss Nancy?" Stuart asked. "It's too loud in here with everyone's chatter."

"Of course, Lieutenant — I mean Stuart."

Stuart held out his arm and Nancy looped hers through it. He led her to the parade grounds and seemed to admire the stars twinkling in the sky. "Miss Nancy, you are as beautiful as this night sky. You have a lot of spunk."

"And you like that in a woman?"

"Oh yes, especially one as beautiful as you."

"You will make me blush, Stuart."

"I only speak the truth. Now, I must ask... do you have a sweetheart at the moment?"

"I couldn't really say if I do or do not — nothing is official."

"Well, that is good news for me," Stuart said, "As I am really taken with you. Do you mind if I kiss you?"

"I don't know if that is a good idea. I hardly know you. We should return to the dance."

"No one will know. Just a little peck on the cheek. Are you telling me you're not interested in me? We could have something quite wonderful. If this man hasn't asked to court you, he may never ask. Maybe he does not feel the same way about you as you do him."

Nancy was silent, pondering Stuart's words. "Well, no he hasn't asked me." Nancy became worried.

"It seems the man you like is not even at the dance. I'm sorry to say it but it doesn't look good. I will court you, Miss Nancy."

"Stuart, as flattering as your offer is, I hardly know you. I am in love with someone else."

"Well, Miss Nancy, what can I say? I am very disappointed," Stuart said with his arms folded. "It's your loss."

Nancy felt insulted and headed back to the dance, leaving Stuart where he was. Clinton arrived and as he was approaching the porch stairs, he saw Nancy walking towards him. "Evening, Nancy. Sorry I am late," Clinton said.

"You're here now, that's the main thing. I haven't seen you for a while. Have you been with Sarah?"

"I have been busy with training, drills, fatigue duties and exercising horses — and no, I haven't been with Sarah. I have been helping her out as she was a visitor to the fort. I can see your skin turning green. Oh yes, you are green with envy." Clinton chuckled.

"Oh, stop it, you cannot blame a girl for being jealous."

"I think we need to dance," said Clinton, and they entered the dining room.

"Oh yes, let's. It doesn't matter if you step on my toes."

"I have a surprise for you, Nancy. I've been practising my dancing."

"Show me, Clinton."

They started dancing, smiling at each other.

"Clinton, I'm so proud. You haven't stepped on my toes yet."

Clinton and Nancy caught a quick glimpse of Lieutenant Mc Ably as he walked in from outside. His face was dumbfounded as he watched Clinton dancing with Nancy. He stormed over to the whiskey. *I wonder what's wrong with him?* Clinton thought and then focused his gaze on Nancy's, feeling as though he could see into her soul. She returned his deep stare.

"I think you better stop looking at me, Nancy. People may think there is something between us."

"I wish there was something between us."

"Why is that?" asked Clinton.

"Because we could be good together — have lots of fun and a bright future."

"Is that so? Well, if I asked your father for permission to court you, what would you say?"

"I would be honoured." Nancy hugged Clinton. She didn't care if that was appropriate or not. She was beyond happy.

"Wait here," said Clinton, who began searching for General Colby through the dancing couples. He was leaning over the piano, giving Marie instructions on what and how to play. Clinton approached General Colby. "Excuse me, General. Can I speak to you for a moment?"

"Yes, Lieutenant. We will step into the kitchen where it is less noisy."

The general led the way into the empty kitchen where he looked at Clinton, encouraging him to speak.

Clinton cleared his throat. "Well, sir... I like your daughter very much and would like your permission to start courting her."

General Colby smiled. "Well, Lieutenant I suppose that is alright. I don't really like the idea of my daughter seeing someone in uniform. It is a dangerous job, but I like you, Clinton, and I know you will do the right thing by my daughter. She has a mind of her own. You know that, don't you?"

"Yes, sir, I know."

"Very well, then, you have my permission."

"Thank you, sir."

Clinton left the kitchen and went straight to Nancy, who was still waiting in the dining area, watching the other dancers. Clinton had a smile on his face as he approached her. "Nancy let's go outside. I've got something to tell you."

They left the dancers and quickly stepped down the porch stairs. "Well, Nancy, your father has given me his permission. So... would you like to court?"

"Yes, yes and yes." Nancy replied, grinning from ear to ear.

"So, Nancy, you are my girl now."

"Hopefully I will become your wife one day."

"Hold on, we have just started courting."

"Yes, I know, but I see a future with you."

Clinton gave Nancy an innocent peck on the check.

"I have to admit that when I saw you with Sarah I was jealous, and then when you didn't show up at the dance on time I thought you weren't coming and didn't have feelings for me. Lieutenant Stuart McAbly approached me and he was so charming and we were dancing. Then we went walking and he tried to kiss me, but nothing happened. It was very bold of him to even suggest it."

"Just because I was helping Sarah doesn't mean I'm interested in her. I was teaching her how to shoot and ride. Her uncle asked me to as she was visiting him with her family. It had to be secret, as he didn't want Sarah's parents to find out — especially her mother."

"I just want to be with you so much, and I don't want you to be with any other woman but me. Oh, Clinton, please forgive me. I adore you so much and I need to be with you."

"Thank you for telling me about what happened. I admit Stuart was out of line but you can't blame him. There is only one belle of the ball," Clinton said, smiling. "Let's take a walk, unless you want to go back and dance?"

"A walk is fine, and you have proved to me that you can dance now so we can dance anywhere."

They walked around the fort grounds with Nancy's arm interwoven in Clinton's — a romantic walk under the twinkling stars. Once they walked into the middle of the parade grounds, Clinton turned to Nancy and asked, "May I have this dance?"

"Of course, sir. I would be honoured."

They started dancing in the wide-open space, a cool breeze brushing their faces. Moonlight trickled down, illuminating them in a sparkling glow. They danced until their feet hurt. They stopped, still holding hands. Something was on Nancy's mind.

"Clinton, I think there is going to be an expedition somewhere — I heard Father talk about it to someone — but I don't know where. You will take me along, won't you? I just couldn't bear being away from you."

"Nancy, I couldn't take you. It is far too dangerous and your father wouldn't dare have you along. Being in the army means being separated from your loved ones for periods of time. No one enjoys being away from their families, but the army calls for it. Are you sure something is being planned?"

"I heard them talking about plans, but I couldn't make out where. I would be a good army wife."

"Why is that?"

"Because I would follow you from the prairie to the mountains to the swamps and beyond."

"Would you really do that?"

"Yes, Clinton. I fell in love with you the first moment I laid eyes on you. I just want to be with you, no matter where you are." Nancy paused for a moment, hoping Clinton would say the same words to her.

"You love me? You actually love me? Wow, that was fast. I didn't think people fell in love that quickly."

"So, Clinton, do you love me too?"

"We have only just started courting. Give me time and let the relationship flourish."

Nancy's shoulders sagged and her head dropped.

"Come on now, don't get upset. I never said that I wouldn't love you or couldn't. I just need time for my feelings to develop."

Nancy nodded in acceptance. There was still hope for her to marry the love of her life.

"Let me walk you back home. Everyone would have left by now. It is getting late and I have to get up early for more drills, but I will see you tomorrow some time."

They slowly walked back, arm in arm. "I don't regret what I said," Nancy remarked. "They are my true feelings and I hope you soon feel the same way. I would be heartbroken if you didn't grow to love me."

"Nancy, did you listen to what I said before? I just need time to discover my feelings, please be patient."

"I am sorry, Clinton. I will give you time."

They arrived at Nancy's residence with no one in sight. All the lamps were turned off, except for one illuminating the hallway. Clinton walked Nancy up the porch stairs. "Goodnight, Nancy, sweet dreams." Clinton kissed her softly on the cheek. He knew Nancy was disappointed that he didn't tell her he loved her.

"Goodnight, Clinton. I will see you tomorrow," Nancy said, feeling vey ecstatic. It had been the best day of her life so far — the night Clinton started courting her. She could only hope and pray that he came to love her.

14

The Vanished

The next morning came quickly. Nancy was still on a high, her smile beaming as she headed downstairs, wearing the brown paisley dress she wore for riding. She was bursting to tell Mamie the terrific news. She really loved her chats with the housekeeper; they could talk about anything.

"Good Morning, Mamie," Nancy said when she entered the kitchen.

Mamie was busy washing dishes from the previous night. "Good Morning, child. How was the social?"

Nancy sat down at the kitchen table. "It was wonderful. The best part was when Clinton asked to court me."

They both squealed with delight.

"You and Clinton are courting?"

"Yes, Mamie. I told him I loved him, but he did not return it yet."

"You did?" Mamie sounded surprised. "Well, child, that was a bit sudden. Maybe he was taken aback by you saying that. I have learnt it is better to wait for a man to say I love you first. It takes men longer to be sure of their feelings. He will fall in love with you, how could he not. Soon you will become Mrs McKay."

"Oh, Mamie, stop it. You will get my hopes up." Nancy blushed and pushed to her feet. "I am going off for an early morning ride and will be back later to have breakfast. I will help you with this mess from last night too. What are we having for breakfast anyway?"

"Eggs and more eggs, anyway you like."

"I like mine scrambled. Bye, Mamie." Nancy headed for the stables. When she got there, Flash was pawing the ground with her right foreleg. "Hello, pretty girl," Nancy said sweetly to her horse. Flash put her head in Nancy's hands and Nancy started scratching her under her chin. "I will feed you when we come back. We are going to be adventurous today and go beyond the fort's walls. You must be sick of me riding you inside all the time. It's still early morning, no one will be around. It will be safe for us to go out quickly. After all, immigrants pass through the fort all the time and nothing happens to them."

Nancy grabbed Flash's bridle and put it on her. Flash was bobbing her head around, eager to stretch her legs. *I think I'll go bareback today. Do something different*, she declared to herself. After all, Nancy was an experienced horsewoman. She'd been around horses all her life. She was just as good as any other experienced male rider — even better.

She led Flash out of the stall and approached an old wooden crate lying in the stable. She hopped onto the crate and gracefully lifted herself onto Flash's back. She held onto the reins and urged Flash on, cantering out of the stables.

Nancy rode Flash out of the fort grounds; flat prairie land stretched to the horizon. She saw a large tree standing alone and thought that would be a good distance to go — only a little way from the fort. She nudged Flash and they galloped towards it. Once they achieved that goal, they became more confident and went a bit further. Nancy had Flash doing figure eight circles. They were both having fun and enjoyed being free of restrictions.

"We should head back now, Flash. I am starving." Nancy urged Flash back towards the fort, her ringlets flew about while dust clouds gathered. Flash galloped back into the fort's entrance, halting outside the stables as Nancy froze with surprise. Clinton was watching her as he watered the horses.

"Nancy! What do you think you are doing?" Clinton demanded.

"Just taking a ride. We didn't go far. We stayed close to the fort."

"You know you are not allowed to leave. Your father would have you arrested if he found out."

"He won't find out. It was just a quick ride. We have been restricted for too long not being able to leave the fort, and it is good for Flash."

"This is not the end of the matter. We will discuss it more, later. Just be careful, okay?"

"You are not my father."

"I am concerned that you don't know the dangers out

there, like rogue Indians and outlaws. Fort Laramie is a thoroughfare for all sorts of unsavoury people. If you want to go out let someone know — myself or your father — so we can arrange some cavalry to protect you."

"My father would never let me go, even if I had the whole regiment with me. I thought we were going to talk about this later. I'm starving, I want to get to breakfast."

"Very well, I will see you later. We have to exercise the horses today. You may be right, there could be something coming up — a long arduous campaign. Here, I'll take Flash for you." Clinton helped Nancy down and took Flash's reins.

"Thank you, Clinton." Nancy walked back to her home quickly, not being able to think of anything but her stomach rumbling. "I am back, Mamie," Nancy said, entering the kitchen. "Oh, good morning, Father and Mother. I have just been out for an early morning ride."

Nancy's father and mother had a worried expression on their faces. They were sitting at the kitchen table, finishing their coffees.

"Sit down, Nancy," instructed the general. "What in the devil were you doing leaving the fort? I have told you before it is too dangerous. One of the lieutenants told me he saw you leave."

"Father, I am not a child. I can look after myself. I stayed close to the fort. There was no harm done. Please don't give me a lecture. Clinton has already spoken to me. Was he the lieutenant who told you?"

"That is confidential."

"Mamie, I would like to eat in my room."

Mamie nodded. "I will bring your breakfast when it is ready."

Nancy turned on her heels and headed to her room, angry that her father was forcing restrictions on her. Ten minutes later, Mamie came into her room with piping hot scrambled eggs and her special homemade biscuits.

"Thank you, Mamie."

"Child, don't be too upset. It is for your own safety. Now, no more sulking. Once you are finished up here I could do with some help tidying up. Your mother is going to give me a hand as well."

"Alright, Mamie."

After breakfast, while the general was attending to his duties, all three women were cleaning, dusting and sweeping. It took them until lunch time to clean everything, and they flopped into the kitchen chairs, needing a well-earned rest. Marie decided to prepare lunch as Mamie looked exhausted. She had been working so hard lately. They gobbled their lunch down and Nancy was desperate to see Clinton, to confront him about telling her father she'd been outside the fort.

She headed off to find him, spotting him exercising a horse near the stables. He was riding a feisty chestnut with white stockings and a white blaze that covered its entire face.

Clinton saw Nancy and steered his horse over to her. "Hello, Nancy. Do you like the look of this horse? I can see it in your eyes. She is just as wild as you are."

"Why did you tell Father?"

"Tell the general what?"

"About what happened this morning?"

"I never said a word to the general. It wasn't me, Nancy. Someone else must have seen you and told him — and rightly so."

"Sorry for accusing you." Nancy petted the horse. "She has lots of spirit, I really like her. I would like to ride her. Does she have a name?"

"The boys have named her Cimarron. She is a pretty little thing but has a mind of her own. The boys think she is one crazy lady."

"Can I ride her now?"

"I don't know," Clinton said, but then he saw the pleading look in Nancy's eyes. "Okay, but just for a couple of minutes before your father comes to check on my progress." Clinton dismounted and gave the reins to Nancy. She adjusted the stirrups and mounted Cimarron.

Nancy started Cimarron on a walk first, before proceeding to trot and then canter. Clinton was gobsmacked at how she had complete control of the horse. All the men that had ridden her had failed to tame her.

Clinton smiled as Nancy steered Cimarron back to him. "I must ask your father if you can take over exercising her, she responds to you. She likes you."

Each morning Nancy exercised Cimarron with her father's permission. Cimarron was becoming much fitter. Her father decided Nancy should keep the horse, since it wouldn't be suitable for long marches and army life, as no one could ride her — apart from Nancy. Nancy had gained a special friend, though she still rode Flash equally as much.

Cimarron and Nancy snuck out of the fort and cantered to the usual spot by the tree. Nancy saw immigrants coming through with wagons and bullocks, horses and cows. The animals looked in bad condition. The people looked even worse. Nancy noticed there was an injured man in the back of one of the wagons.

"Excuse me, miss. Is there a doctor at the fort?" asked a female immigrant with a German accent, nursing the injured man.

"Yes, ma'am, there is an army surgeon. What happened?"

"We were ambushed by Indians and an arrow shaft is stuck in his leg. We couldn't get it out."

"Doctor Porter is his name and he has quarters by the barracks. Good luck to you."

Nancy wanted to finish her ride, and decided she would help the immigrants once she was done. Away she went, being more daring and riding past the tree. Cimarron had her ears pricked and was enjoying the freedom. Nancy was enjoying herself as well — having the wind flowing through her tight curls, making them bounce. Nancy was so swept up in being free, she didn't realise she'd travelled further than she should have. She turned Cimarron around to go back when...

Clinton hadn't seen Nancy all morning, which was quite

unusual as they would always bump into each other at some point. Clinton approached the general's quarters. Mamie was sweeping the front porch. "Hello, Lieutenant," she said.

"Good morning, Mamie. Have you seen Nancy?"

"No, I haven't. Sometimes she goes off for early morning rides and has a late breakfast. I assumed she was with you somewhere. But now that I think about it, she should have been back by now." Mamie started to become worried.

"I will go back to the stables and check if her horses are there," said Clinton.

"Should I inform the general?" asked Mamie.

"Not just yet. She must be somewhere creating havoc."

Clinton left Mamie and approached the stables. He noticed Flash was there but not Cimarron. *Nancy must be riding, but she's not around the fort.* Suddenly it occurred to him that she must have ridden outside the fort. Clinton's stomach knotted. He wandered from the stables and spotted newly arrived immigrants unpacking their supplies. *Perhaps they'd seen her riding outside*, Clinton thought.

He approached a woman. "Excuse me, ma'am. On your travels through did you see a young blonde woman on a chestnut horse?"

"Yes, we did as we were approaching the fort. I asked her if there was a doctor around because one of our people had an arrow embedded in his leg. The doctor is operating now and is not sure if he will be able to save the leg, so we are staying inside the fort until he is fit to travel."

"I'm sorry to hear that, ma'am. Did you see anyone else near the fort?"

"No, there was no one else around."

"Much obliged, ma'am, for your information." Clinton thought it was time to report to General Colby. He surveyed the fort and spotted the general in the parade ground, conducting drills with some raw recruits. He quickly made his way over there.

"Excuse me, General Colby, I need to talk to you about something urgent."

General Colby dismissed the recruits before turning to Clinton. "What is it, Lieutenant?"

"I cannot find Nancy anywhere, and I am concerned something has happened. Apparently, she was riding Cimarron outside the fort. She should have been back by now. Something is wrong — very wrong. Can I have your permission to leave and look for her?"

"Damn it! Nancy is so stubborn — she has a mind of her own. And you have looked for her everywhere?"

"Yes, General. If she was back Cimarron would be at the stables."

"Oh dear, God. If anything has happened to her... I could never face Marie again."

"General, we need to organise a search party."

"Inform Captain Larsen to organise thirty soldiers to go west and another thirty to go east. I will take command of one and he the other."

"Yes, sir." Clinton ran off to inform Captain Larsen, who got started on organising the soldiers.

Clinton and the other twenty-nine cavalry were following

General Colby over the prairie, heading east, but so far there was no sign of Nancy. Clinton rode up to the general. "General, I ask your permission to act as a scout and ride in front of the company — it might be quicker that way to spot her."

"Very well but take three men with you. We don't know what is out there. And, Lieutenant, keep a cool head. If you don't, it could get you into trouble. Oh, I just hope we find her. I haven't told Marie yet. I'm really worried. I shouldn't have given her that horse."

"General, it will be okay. We will find her."

Hours passed, but there was no Nancy, no horse and no evidence that there had been a struggle. The general showed emotional strain. He was fighting back tears that were threatening to flow. He'd led the cavalry into the middle of nowhere — the land was endless. The command halted and the general sent a messenger to inform Clinton and the three other soldiers to come back.

Captain Larsen circled around to try and find General Colby and his outfit before it was dark. He eventually spotted them and trotted to the general, his command following behind.

"General, the horses are getting tired. Perhaps we should start again in the morning? We only have a couple of daylight hours left," said Captain Larsen.

"Captain Larsen, don't tell me what to do. I need to find my daughter. She is my only child. I need to find her. This will kill my wife. Oh, God, what if I never see her again?"

"General, we have searched all the ground that we could possibly search. We won't give up hope, but let's turn back and start again in the morning. It is the only way. Your wife will be worried."

The General nodded in defeat and both companies headed back to Fort Laramie, exhausted.

Clinton walked into the forts grounds after filling his belly. It had been a long day of searching for Nancy. He wanted time to himself. He looked to the night sky and concentrated on one particular shining star, yelling, "Where are you, Nancy? God, please show us the way. We need to find her, please."

Clinton dropped to his knees and started crying. He knew things weren't looking good for Nancy. He needed a miracle.

The next morning couldn't come quick enough. The cavalry was ready to continue the search with more men this time, and Indian scouts they'd hired. They divided into three groups, searching and searching until...

An Indian scout got off his horse and noticed scuff marks on the dusty ground. He looked at it more closely. "What is it? Have you found something?" The general asked eagerly, using a form of sign language common across the plains.

The scout replied, pointing to the ground, indicating there were horse shoe marks. It looked as though there were six different sets, indicating six horsemen. The scout raised six fingers to represent the horsemen.

"Can we follow these tracks?" the general asked using sign language again.

The scout nodded.

Clinton was right behind the general, and could barely contain his glee that they'd finally found something that could help them locate Nancy.

"Clinton, inform Captain Larsen that we have found tracks and they should follow us. We may come across an Indian village. She is alive! She is alive!"

"Yes, sir." Clinton steered Ranger away to find Captain Larsen.

The scouts took off, following the tracks, which led them down a hidden ravine and through to a hidden creek. Everyone stopped to let their horses drink, giving the horses a brief rest while still mounted, before continuing to ride, following the creek. To their amazement they came across an empty Indian village with nothing in sight, apart from tepee circles indented into the ground.

One of the scouts tried to communicate with the general about the Indian village that had been there. He used a stick to draw a picture of a tepee in the dirt and pointed in the direction of where the Indians had probably headed.

"What are we waiting for? Let's proceed," said General Colby, following the scouts from the abandoned village.

The cavalry spent the next four days searching, camping under the stars every night, but the general's deep devotion to finding his daughter made him neglect important facts.

On the fifth day, in the early morning while they were still at the camp, Captain Larsen approached General Colby, who was inspecting his horse's hooves. "General, food is becoming drastically low, as is water. This is our fifth day today and we haven't seen any Indians. How long are you going to look? We never expected to be out this long. If Nancy was in this area we would have found her. I am sorry, sir."

"Captain, do you know what calling off the search actually means? It means that I have stopped looking for my daughter, that there is no more hope and that she will never come home. While I'm searching there is hope."

"General, I am sorry but a decision has to be made. If we carry on like this you may lose more than your daughter. There are men and horses to think about. You don't want them to perish out here."

"Stop it! I know my responsibilities."

Captain Larsen nodded and left him alone. The general looked out at the bare flat plains and spoke to the men. "Men, whoever wants to return to Fort Laramie may do so. I am giving myself more time to search for my daughter. She is here somewhere and whoever stays will receive double wages."

Most of the cavalry turned back. They were hungry, exhausted and wanted to return to the fort's safety. They feared the general's desperation could lead him to make rash decisions that could endanger their lives.

Only twenty men remained, including Clinton and Captain Larsen, as well as the Indian scouts whom the general had persuaded with the promise of a large amount of supplies.

"Much regards, men," General Colby said. "We will make camp for the night."

Once Clinton had finished helping set up the camp, he approached General Colby, who was looking at the horizon, smoking his pipe. "General, I am happy to search with you as long as it takes."

"Much obliged, Lieutenant. I am glad you are here as when we find Nancy, she will probably need you."

Clinton nodded, not really understanding what he meant. He feared Nancy was lost forever, but he hoped he was wrong.

Daybreak had arrived and everyone was ready to start the day. The scouts led the way, with the general not that far behind. They covered a lot of ground that day, but still no Nancy. The general was so disappointed he couldn't speak. There was no evidence, nothing at all. All his hopes and dreams of finding Nancy vanished. It was time to let go. It was time to say goodbye. It was time to grieve.

Once the soldiers had made a new camp in the vicinity of the never ending plains, he gathered the men around the camp and announced they were heading back. It wasn't an easy decision to make. He was heartbroken.

Clinton was stunned. "Are you sure, General, that you want to turn back? I will stay with you and keep searching if you want. We both have the strongest horses."

The general continued his speech. "I am sure. There

is nothing here. We haven't found anything, not even a speck of evidence — only tracks that led us to dead ends. Where is she? I do not know. Is she alive? I do not know. Has she suffered a cruel fate? I do not know. I have tried to find her, but I cannot search among the plains forever. I don't want to give up, but sometimes, you have to be realistic and say this is not working. I'm going around in circles. It is time to go back to the fort. Marie will be beside herself with worry and now I am coming back without Nancy. She will never forgive me for bringing her and Nancy out here. Our marriage won't be the same."

Tears had welled in the general's eyes. He tried to hide them from his men, but one trickled down his left cheek. All the soldiers were silent, not knowing what to say. Clinton was heartbroken, his chest and throat tight. He felt that Nancy, his sweet shining light, was gone forever.

A week had passed and General Colby and Marie decided to have a memorial service for Nancy. The blacksmith at the fort had created a plaque to commemorate her life, placing it near the stables' entrance, where she had spent most of her time. The memorial was conducted at the fort's parade ground, which every soldier attended out of respect for General Colby.

Marie couldn't stop crying. The General, Clinton and Mamie spoke about Nancy's life. There were many tears. There was silence once all the speeches had been conducted. The attendees started to trickle back to their army duties. The General, Marie and Mamie walked slowly back to their quarters, wiping the tears as they trickled down their faces. Each step they took was enveloped by pain. Clinton walked towards Nancy's plaque and stayed there in silence, remembering everything about her: her smile, her dancing green eyes, her cheekiness and what could have been. Would she have been his wife? Out of the corner of his eye, he saw an unusual wildflower growing a few feet from where he was standing. He picked it up and placed it on Nancy's memorial plaque and without hesitating he said, "I love you, Nancy."

15

The Goodbye and the Surprise

A year and a half had gone by at Fort Laramie since Nancy's disappearance. General Colby had something important to tell Clinton. They were both sitting on the dining room chairs in the general's residence, drinking coffee. Clinton was fiddling with his tin cup while General Colby spoke.

"Clinton, I want to thank you for all of your support during this trying time. You just sitting with Marie has helped her. She is struggling with the loss of our daughter and I am trying to do the best I can, but I have decided to move to New York. I have to get Marie out of here. She cannot move on when she is here. She stares out the back window every day, waiting for Nancy's return. It breaks my heart to see her this way. This is my only option. I need to save my wife," said General Colby.

"I am glad I could help you and your wife. I believe you're right, that she was much better when someone was there with her. I think she felt comfort with people who knew Nancy. There are still a lot of questions to what happened to Nancy — the not knowing is the one thing that will bring you down. It will always be on our minds. General, I think it is a good idea to take Marie somewhere different, a new environment. How did she take the news of leaving the fort?"

"She cried, and told me Nancy might come back and she has to be here, but Mamie and I convinced her that she wasn't coming back. She cried and cried, but I think she has come to realise that it is for the best and hasn't said a word about it since. We are starting to pack things now. We will only take the essentials and leave most things here for the next general."

"What do you think you will do in New York?" asked Clinton.

"I have an appointment with General Sherman when I arrive, so hopefully he will give me a position of some sort. There will be no more frontier work for me. Speaking of the frontier, I am promoting you to captain. I have the power to do that. I know you have only been in the army for a little while, but you have shown leadership skills, which is sometimes hard to find. All the men like you, and you have done so much for Marie and me. You have shown me what type of man you are."

"General, I am honoured that you think of me that way, and I am forever grateful for the promotion. I would like to continue my career in the army, even though the conditions are tough. I think everything changed once I was in the Civil War. My mindset changed and I got used to roughing it, I suppose. I cannot really see what else I could do. I think the army is part of me now, unless I become fearful of going into battle, that is when I know I will have to resign. Do I fear dying out there? Absolutely. But, then again, even if you have a dangerous occupation sometimes that is not what gets you. It is being in unfamiliar territory."

"What do you mean, Clinton?"

"General, my familiar territory is out on the plains. I understand the Indians' tactics in warfare, the perils of the open spaces, the wild animals that surround us. Unfamiliar territory would be out on the ocean. I have never been on the water and don't know how to swim. What I am saying is that things you don't know could get you into trouble. No one has control of where their fate lies, and what is meant to be will be. You see and understand that more when you are in battle. The soldier right next to you is alive one moment and then a bullet or arrow shoots through their head."

"Yes, life is very unpredictable on the frontier, but, Clinton, just live your life the best way you can. I suppose you are right in one way, just because you are in the army doesn't mean you will be at the mercy of it. Look at me, I have a few scars but I survived and I know it is time for me to give it up. No regrets. When I get settled I will send my details to you so if you are ever that way, you are most welcome to visit, even if the years have passed. I am not sure what Mamie is going to do if she decides to stay on with her two daughters. If there is any news about Nancy, no matter how small, please contact me. I will speak to the next general when he is appointed and tell him about the situation and leave my details with him."

"Very well, sir. I wish you all the best. When do you leave?"

"Three days' time. You are the first one I have told, apart from the senior officials. It has been in the works for a while. Captain Larsen will warm the spot for the next general — the war department may even make it permanent."

Three days later, in the early morning, General Colby and his wife left the fort on a stagecoach. They didn't look back, nor did they look forward; they looked down in sorrow, holding each other's hands and leaving the destination that took their beloved daughter. This was the time when they had to say goodbye to Nancy forever and create a new life; otherwise grief would consume their souls.

They moved on to start afresh, but they left so many unanswered questions on the frontier — a lot of 'what if's' that remained on the wind's breath to eternity. They were whispers among the prairie.

Clinton was preparing for his first day as captain. He was up at dawn at the front entrance of the fort, looking at the horizon. Today was his first patrol in command. He had mixed emotions of excitement, nervousness and doubtfulness about whether he was ready to take on this position. He had to be quick in making decisions and instructing his men if they were caught in an ambush. *Why am I doubting myself? I can do this. I have fought Indians before and know what tricks they can pull over us. I know the plains now and how the weather can quickly change. I know where the creek beds are for water. I can do this. I can command and look after my men.*

Why are you doubting yourself, Clinton? Clinton thought to himself. He went back to the stables where the men were saddling horses and preparing for their routine patrol. There was much noise: horses were neighing and stamping their feet and men were chattering. *You can do this,* Clinton told himself. *You can do this.* Clinton was pleased that Captain Larsen was promoted to General.

Ten months after Clinton became a captain, a chestnut horse with white stockings appeared on the horizon. It stood still and surveyed its surroundings, nostrils flaring as it sniffed the air. It reared up on its hind legs and punched its forelegs in the air before sprinting like lightning into the fort, where it pranced around, snorting and neighing.

Clinton was outside the stables attending to Ranger's hooves when he heard all the commotion and made his way over to the horse. "Oh my... Is that you, Cimarron? Is that really you? Hey, Jacob, can you grab me a rope halter. Cimarron is back." Clinton stroked her neck. "It is alright, girl. You are safe. We will look after you. Where have you been?" Clinton looked into Cimarron's eyes and saw fear. She was not the same horse as she used to be. Her spirit had changed; Clinton could see it in her eyes. Cimarron nestled her head into Clinton's arms.

"Here you go, sir." Jacob handed him a rope halter. "I cannot believe it's her. Where has she come from?"

"I don't know." Clinton slipped the halter onto her. "I will put her in the stalls and she can rest. She looks tired.

I have no idea where she has been. It has been two years since... you know. This is a miracle."

"Should we send word to General Colby?"

"Not at the moment. I will tell General Larsen. The horse did come back but it doesn't mean Nancy is alive, and I am actually glad that General Colby and Marie didn't see Cimarron's return. They would never have left the fort. When we are on patrol, we will do some scouting and see what we can come up with."

After putting Cimarron in the stalls, Clinton went straight to General Larsen's quarters to explain the situation and to get permission for a patrol. General Larsen agreed on the condition they would return in four hours. Clinton chose fifteen men, including Jacob, to search the prairie lands for any sign that Nancy was alive.

After four hours, they had found nothing and Clinton returned to the fort disheartened. The next step was to see Cimarron. The resident vet, Doctor Mac, had fallen ill and wasn't available, so Clinton decided to examine Cimarron himself for any clues about where she had come from.

He picked up her legs and noticed there were no shoes on her hoofs. Her mouth was fairly soft, indicating there had been no metal bits placed in it. She had a scar on her left shoulder that hadn't been there before she vanished. She seemed so quiet and docile — the opposite to how she was before. She had fighting spirit, but now her spirit was broken. Tears welled in Clinton's eyes. He looked at Cimarron and felt a connection to Nancy that gave him hope again.

Clinton was at the stables early the next morning. He was still intrigued about Cimarron. He stared at the horse, hoping to read her mind and find answers — if only horses could talk. "Good morning, Jacob," he said when his friend walked in.

"Good morning, Captain. How is she?"

"She is a changed horse. She seems so despondent. Can you take Cimarron to see Dr Mac? I think he is on duty now. I am so glad we have a vet at this fort. Let me know what he says."

"Yes, sir. I will take her now."

Jacob led Cimarron to an open stall at the back of the stables, which was connected to Dr Mac's office — a small room kept impeccably neat. Jacob found Dr Mac washing his hands in a bucket at the corner of the stall, having just sutured a wounded horse's leg.

"Dr Mac, I have a patient for you. I don't know what is wrong, she is despondent. This horse was the one Nancy rode before she disappeared, and the horse suddenly showed up yesterday. Can you take a look at her?" Jacob asked.

"Of course, Lieutenant." He wiped his wet hands on a towel. "So, she just appeared yesterday? Has she been eating?"

"Not that much."

"Hold her still while I have a look." Dr Mac examined her body, lifting her legs, pinching around her muscles and looking inside her mouth. His hands went all over her body, feeling every inch for any abnormalities. "I cannot find any health concerns with her. She needs to be fattened up a bit but, otherwise, she is in good order. Her despondence likely has something to do with what happened to her out there. Something changed her. I do remember her when she first arrived. She was so flighty — no one could ride her — and now she is as docile as a kitten. Give her time, let her rest and see how she is then. Very slowly reintroduce oats into her meals, but for now keep her on pasture and hay. If she doesn't improve, come back and see me."

"Thanks, Doc. I will inform my captain." Jacob led Cimarron back to Clinton, who was still at the stables and told him what the vet had said.

"Well, I suppose all we can do is give her some rest and see if she improves. Maybe the doc is right, that she has been mentally scarred. All the signs point to her being an Indian horse — that scar on her shoulder could have been from an arrow, the soft mouth indicates she hasn't had a bit in her mouth and she has unshod feet. All of this makes it clear she's been with the Indians. When I first joined the army, an old chap told me that cavalry horses react differently to Indians, and Indian horses react differently to Whites. There must be something significant in that. You can just imagine the Indians whooping and yelling, and how frightening that must be for horses not used to that."

"We get scared ourselves when we hear Indian cries — they certainly know how to unnerve the enemy. Once she feels safe she may come well again," said Jacob.

"Let's hope so. She is such a beautiful animal and deserves a second chance."

General Larsen walked into the stables, spotting Clinton. He handed him a crumpled piece of paper. "Captain McKay, there is a message from headquarters to all captains. How is Cimarron doing?"

"I don't know exactly. She has been vet checked and he said she needs time to readjust."

"Should we inform General Colby now?" asked General Larsen.

"Yes, I think so, but tell them there is no evidence of Nancy being alive. I don't want them to get their hopes up," said Clinton.

"I will inform all companies to be on the lookout. I will organise a letter to be sent to the Colby's. I will leave you to it, Captain and Lieutenant Butler."

Clinton unravelled the crumpled telegram. He read it privately.

"What does it say, Clinton? Or is it secret army business?" asked Jacob.

"It states that the seventh cavalry are looking for experienced captains for their upcoming campaign."

"Why couldn't they promote one of their own to captaincy instead of taking captains from other divisions?" asked Jacob, disgruntled.

"I suppose they may only have raw recruits who are not suitable. But I have to say, I am not entirely experienced as a captain."

"Experience doesn't count for everything. The men really do respect you, and you can't buy respect. Are you thinking of applying for this position?"

"No, I like it here and I feel close to Nancy when I am amongst the plains."

"That is good news. I don't want you to leave. Fort Laramie needs you."

"Thanks, Jacob, and for your friendship." Clinton folded the telegram and placed it in his pocket. A fresh opportunity had fallen into his hands. Would it change his life forever or did the spirit of Nancy have too much control over him?

Two weeks had passed and Clinton was walking towards the stables. He reached in his pocket, finding the telegram General Larsen had given him. He had forgotten all about it. His mind had been entirely on Nancy and Cimarron. His gut told him to keep searching but his head told him to stop as it had proven futile in the past. *But what if she's alive?* His mind worked overtime and the only thing that kept him sane was his work.

Jacob bumped into Clinton and the telegram fell on the ground. "Jacob, what are you doing? Remember to look straight ahead when you are carrying a load."

"Sorry, Captain. I am a bit clumsy today. I should know not to pile all my riding gear on top of the saddle as I am not that tall. You have dropped a bit of paper. Is that the telegram? You are considering leaving, aren't you?"

Clinton picked up the telegram. "It just fell out of my pocket. I forgot it was there. I haven't even thought about it. I have been thinking of Nancy lately and if she is alive out there. Maybe Cimarron came back to tell us something."

"Like what? I think your imagination has gone wild. It has been just over two years. She could be anywhere now — if she's alive."

"I don't know, Jacob. I really don't know where to look."

"Look? What do you mean look? You are not considering going out there again, are you?"

"I have been thinking about it. I will take Cimarron and let her run free and she can lead me."

"What?! Clinton, listen to me. You don't know that Cimarron will return to where she came from. She may want to avoid the whole area. If Nancy is in an Indian village, and that is a big if, what would you do? You can't go in there with guns blazing and demand Nancy back."

"I could sneak in under nightfall."

"Clinton, this is crazy talk. If you enter an Indian village, you will not come out." Jacob shook his head. "What are we saying? We are talking as though Nancy is alive and being held captive."

"I believe that's the truth. Nancy was a pretty girl. I am sure that whatever Indian tribe took her, kept her. I don't believe she is dead, not anymore. When we followed those Indian horse tracks we came to dead ends. I think the Indians misled us on purpose, and maybe they thought we would conduct a search and that is why the village wasn't there. They got out pretty quickly."

"Clinton, that is wishful thinking. We have searched to no end. It is so hard to find Indians — you need Indians to track Indians. If this situation is really affecting you, maybe you should consider this new job."

"I really like it here at the fort. There is always something happening and you meet a lot of colourful characters. I have a good relationship with the men. If I went somewhere new I would have to start over again building relationships."

"Is that such a bad thing though? Starting somewhere new and meeting new people? You might even like it where you are going. It will probably be pretty similar to here, and I hear the seventh cavalry is starting to build a bit of a reputation as a tight fighting outfit. I suppose one bad side is General Custer, who is rumoured to be hard on his men, but don't let that put you off."

"Jacob, it sounds as if you want to get rid of me. I thought you wanted me to stay. And my friend Tom is actually General Custer's brother. I am pretty sure that Tom is in the seventh cavalry with his brother."

"I do want you to stay, but I don't want you to stay because of your wishful thinking about Nancy being alive. You are hanging on to the past, Clinton."

"I really feel in my heart that she is out there somewhere. Cimarron gave me hope, but I don't know where to look. Maybe we are looking in the wrong area and we need months to get to where we need to be."

"I assume the seventh cavalry is preparing for a big campaign and that is why they are asking for captains, and I am sure they will come in contact with the Indians. Maybe this is your chance to go to another area and see if there are white captives among them. Maybe Nancy isn't here but somewhere else. I can't believe I am saying this now, you've got me believing she is alive."

"When you put it like that it sounds as though I should go, but I might not be appointed to the position there. There are a lot more experienced captains out there."

"Not every captain is going to apply so you have a chance. I am sure General Colby will put in a good word for you, even General Larsen. So it's settled, you are going to tell General Larsen that you wish to apply."

"Alright, I will do it."

16

New Opportunity

Two weeks later Clinton was ready to part for new territory, new adventures and new danger. Clinton was at the front of the fort, ready to embark on the stagecoach. Ranger was, of course, coming with him too. Their bond was unbreakable; they couldn't leave each other now. Clinton tied Ranger to the back of the coach while Jacob loaded Clinton's gear on the roof.

"Jacob, stay in touch and take good care of Cimarron and Flash," Clinton said, approaching his friend. "Those horses are both yours now and I imagine you could probably use Cimarron out on patrol. She is just about ready to embark on being a mount, and it's probably a good idea to have both Flash and Cimarron together in the same outfit as they would enjoy each other's company. I trust you with them and they both like you, I can tell."

"Thank you, Clinton. I will treat both of them well. I will miss you — the fort won't be the same. Look after yourself."

"We will meet again, and you can always transfer over if you desire a change."

They hugged each other in respect and knew the chances of seeing each other again were very slim.

This was it now. Clinton's new journey awaited and he had to get to Fort Hays as soon as possible.

It took Clinton a few more days than expected to arrive at his new post. He would have been lost without his trusty stead. They were at the entrance of Fort Hays. "Look, Ranger, we made it. Thank Heavens for that. There is a good meal of hay and chaff waiting for you, maybe some oats." Ranger neighed and his pace became more fluent. "Gee, Ranger, the fort looks deserted. What is going on? You stay here while I find someone." Clinton dismounted. Ranger neighed and stamped his foot. "Don't worry, I haven't forgotten about your meal." Ranger neighed again.

Clinton walked to the stables, there were only a handful of horses. He heard a rustle in the back corner and spotted someone spreading fresh hay. "Hello there. My name is Captain Clinton McKay. I'm here to join the seventh cavalry."

"You've missed them by six hours, Captain. They knew you were coming but they couldn't wait. They thought something had happened to you. They have headed to Camp Supply. I can lend you a horse and you can make your way."

"Thank you for the offer, but I'd prefer to take my own horse."

"I am Burkman, sir. General Custer's groom. Just call me Burks — that's my nickname. You've had a long journey, your horse needs to rest. Let me look after him until you depart."

"Pleasure to meet you, Burks. I would be grateful for you looking after my horse. I think he's hungry and would love a good feed and back rub."

"Leave it to me, Captain. Get some rest yourself, there are plenty of spare bunks."

"Much obliged, Burks."

After a day's rest, Ranger and Clinton made their way towards Camp Supply, following Burkman's instructions on how to get there. Clinton's body felt tired and achy. He held on to Ranger's neck as he closed his eyes. His face was flushed. "Are we there yet, Ranger?"

Ranger was silent. There was still a while to go. After travelling a few more hours, they finally saw the outskirts of Camp Supply. Clinton felt a bit better and pepped himself up to make a good impression. He rode through the camp. "Where is General Custer?" Clinton asked a lieutenant attending to the horses.

"Just over yonder, sir, in the second tent to the right."

"Much obliged, Lieutenant." Clinton dismounted Ranger and took a deep breath, clearing his throat before entering the tent, finding General Custer folding a letter. "General Custer, I am Captain Clinton McKay reporting for service, sir." He saluted.

"Where have you been? We thought the Indians may have scalped you, that's why we left without you. You are very brave to have travelled through enemy territory alone."

"I have a good horse, sir, who can sense when Indians are around. I was going to ask if you have come across any white female captives. An important person named Nancy Colby went missing at Fort Laramie. She had blonde curls and green eyes."

"Well, Captain, you seem to have plenty of experience dealing with Indian warriors and to my recall there has been no woman of that description,"

Clinton's heart sank. *No Nancy.* "Yes, sir, a few skirmishes on the Bozeman Trail."

"Well, you have more experience than most of my men."

Clinton nodded in respect. "General, I hope you don't mind me asking, but I was a friend of your brother's, Tom. We were in the Civil War together. I was wondering if he was here with you, sir?"

"Well, Captain, if you turn around you can ask him yourself."

Tom had just entered the tent.

"Tom!" Clinton exclaimed.

"Oh my, Clinton, what are you doing here?"

"I am part of the seventh cavalry now."

They both hugged each other like long lost friends.

"I cannot believe you are here," said Tom. "And you have met the good old general. He is not bad for an older brother, and not too bad for a general, but if he gives you any trouble just let me know as he can be a ruffian at times."

"Oh, Tom, cut it out," the general said. "You'll give the captain here the wrong impression."

"See, Clint, I told you he was trouble."

Everyone burst into laughter.

"You're still as jovial as ever, Tom."

"You have to be to survive army life."

"Captain McKay, as you know my brother, you can share his tent and, Tom, I will let you get him acquainted. Give him the run down."

"Come on, Clint. Let's go." Tom led Clinton from General Custer's tent to his own — a short walk away. "Well, Clint here is my wonderful home. I'll get you some army rations. Make yourself comfortable."

"Thanks, Tom," Clinton said and approached the tent. To his surprise, a young wolf, about ten months, jumped out and nipped his heels, growling. "Easy, boy, calm down. What are you doing here?" Clinton noticed the wolf was on a long chain. "What is Tom doing with you? I think I'll stay right here." Clinton stood still for a few minutes trying to get the wolf to calm down. Clinton could see Tom approaching and laughing.

"That is my pet wolf, Dakota," Tom explained. "Easy, boy, you can back down now." The wolf backed away. "You can go in, Clinton."

"Are you sure it's not going to eat me when I go into the tent?"

"He might try. I'm not sure I fed him today." Tom grinned.

Clinton ran into the tent before the wolf could attack. He breathed a sigh of relief to be away from it, but then he heard a strange rattling sound. He approached the end of the tent and noticed a couple of square boxes covered with a cloth. He lifted the cloth and gasped in horror when he saw rattlesnakes hissing.

"Tom! Tom!" Clinton yelled.

"What's wrong, Clint?" He walked into the tent. "Oh! You have met my prize collection of rattlers. Just be nice to them and they won't get you."

Clinton was worried, but Tom was grinning from ear to ear. "Tom, what is going on here? Are you creating a zoo?"

"Well, two of my prized rattlesnakes have, in fact, been sent to England to be placed in a zoo."

"I don't think there is enough room for me in here."

"Of course there is. At the back, where the rattlers are, there is room."

"Very funny. I think I may sleep outside with the wolf."

"I wouldn't recommend that. He might get hungry during the night."

"I think I might set up my own tent."

"Well, if you think that's best."

"I do. I won't get any sleep in here."

It was a restless night for Clinton. His whole body ached, his chest was congested and he couldn't stop shaking. He was miserable. The Reveille sounded, but he couldn't move from the floor of his tent.

Tom walked in. "Clinton, are you alright? Oh, you look horrible."

Clinton replied in a husky voice, "I feel awful. I don't feel I'll be able to get out of bed. The cold is going through to my bones."

"I will inform the general. I'll be back in a minute." Tom walked briskly to his brother's tent. He sensed something was seriously wrong with Clinton. General Custer was standing outside his tent, drinking coffee while surveying the horizon. "General, Captain McKay is as sick as a dog. He requires a doctor."

"Very well. You will need to send him to Fort Cobb. Arrange the military wagon and an escort and round up any other sick men. I cannot have anyone on board that is not at full capacity, nothing can spoil this operation. General Sherman is counting on me to get results. Hitch their horses to the wagons. Once they are well, they will need to return on their own accord," General Custer informed his brother.

Tom nodded and went about making arrangements.

They left for Fort Cobb at dusk. There were five other men on board the wagon, including Clinton, who was the sickest. He was alternating between having a fever, and the shivers. They finally made it to Fort Cobb in the early evening. The ill soldiers were put in a spare dormitory for the sick. Clinton was put in a back room, as the doctor believed he was contagious. He dosed him with cough medicine and whiskey every four hours– an old remedy to kill germs lurking in the body.

The doctor walked into Clinton's room that evening. Clinton was lying in bed with his eyes closed, trying to fall asleep.

"Can you hear me, young chap?" the doctor asked. Clinton's eyes fluttered open and he nodded. "You have a bad dose of influenza, which I suppose is better to have than small pox or cholera. Even though you are mighty sick, you still have a fighting chance. You are young and strong. Stay in bed. I will see you tomorrow."

Five days later, Clinton was sitting up. He still felt weak and intoxicated, due to the doctor pouring whiskey down his throat constantly. He felt disappointed that he wasn't doing his duty at the fort. Time would tell whether this was a blessing in disguise.

17

The Meeting

After ten days at Fort Cobb, Clinton had been passed fit to travel back to Camp Supply. He was sitting up on his bunk bed in the dormitory while the fort doctor reassessed his condition, making doubly sure he was fit enough to travel through the rough cold weather. "Captain, I cannot see a reason why you shouldn't go back. I think you are ready for service, but only on light duties. I will write a note to give to your commanding officer. You mentioned something about a campaign coming up. On doctor's orders, I don't think you should go due to the weather and the endurance of the campaign. You may relapse."

"Thanks, Doc. I will keep that in mind. I'm itching to get back. Much obliged for the great care you gave me."

"That is my job, Captain. Some people don't survive a horrible influenza. You came in at the right time. If you'd arrived a day later, you probably would have contracted pneumonia and there would have been nothing I could have done. Take care of yourself."

"Bye, Doc. Thanks for everything." The doctor gave Clinton the written letter and left.

Clinton felt like some fresh air and left the dormitory, walking around the perimeter to make sure he felt fit enough to ride back today. As Clinton looked at the snow-covered horizon, he saw a group of riders approaching; they were Indians — five of them. Clinton decided he wanted to meet and greet them, something different than the usual hostilities. He made his way to the fort entrance as the riders were approaching. Clinton raised his hand in a friendly gesture, hoping they would understand he was trying to say hello, and in sign language he tried to ask if they needed help.

They all had their buffalo robes high up around their necks, covering most of their face, blocking out the chill of the air. One of the Indians lowered their robe, revealing a beautiful woman with satin hair. "Hello," she said. "My name is Morning Dove, and this is our great chief Black Kettle. My other tribe members are Buffalo Runs, Little Eagle and Jumps The Water.

Clinton was gobsmacked. "You speak English? What brings you here in this horrible weather?"

"We are here to see Colonel Hazen. It is important for Black Kettle to see him. I am translating and the others are here for support."

"I will try and find him for you. Why don't you all take your horses to the stables and take shelter there. Follow me."

Morning Dove and the other Indians dismounted their horses and followed Clinton to the stables where she turned to Black Kettle and spoke in her native tongue. Black Kettle held out his hand in a token of friendship to Clinton.

"Thank you for welcoming us. You never told us your name," said Morning Dove.

"I am Captain Clinton McKay — just call me Clinton. I cannot believe you speak English. How did you learn?"

"From George Bent, a friend of Black Kettle's."

"Yes, Black Kettle's name is known through the ranks, as well as other famous chiefs such as Red Cloud and Sitting Bull. You speak so well. You interpret for your tribe?"

"Yes, Black Kettle likes to take me along when we have to talk to the army. He trusts me and knows I will interpret correctly."

"I will go and find some warm drinks — you must be frozen — and find the Colonel for you. Stay here. I will be back shortly."

Morning Dove nodded, and the Indians stayed inside the stables, holding their horses and speaking in their native tongue.

Clinton went into the officers' quarters and found Colonel Hazen sitting at his desk, signing papers. Clinton knocked on the open door. "Excuse me Colonel."

"Yes, what is it?"

"Chief Black Kettle is here to see you with a handful of followers."

"Why do they want to see me?"

"I'm not sure, sir, but they wouldn't have travelled all this way if it wasn't important. They are waiting at the stables. I told them they could stay there. Would you like me to escort them to your quarters?"

"No, don't do that. I will go and meet them shortly — in about twenty minutes."

"Very well, sir." Clinton left while Colonel Hazen continued signing his papers.

Clinton decided to go to the mess hall next and boil some water on the black wood fired stove to make coffee for his new-found friends. He retrieved a robust silver tray and placed the tin cups on it, walking quickly to the stables before the coffee could cool.

"Here we go. I brought coffee," Clinton said, re-entering the stables. He passed the tin cups around but the Indians were hesitant to drink.

"We don't drink coffee," Morning Dove explained. "It's not part of our diet but we will try it." Morning Dove translated what the drink was and to try it. They all took a sip at the same time and quickly spat it out. "Clinton, I am sorry, but the taste is too strong. We appreciate the trouble you went through to bring it."

"Sorry, I'm not the best coffee maker." Clinton gathered the cups and poured them onto the snow-covered ground. He spotted Colonel Hazen walking towards the stables, "It looks like the colonel is coming now," Clinton told Morning Dove. Colonel Hazen walked arrogantly into the entrance of the stables. "Colonel Hazen, sir, I would like to introduce Black Kettle, Buffalo Runs, Little Eagle, Jumps The Water and Morning Dove — she is an interpreter."

"Captain, you didn't have to introduce me to everyone, just who I am going to talk to." Clinton didn't say anything. "Alright, I haven't got all day. Who is going to talk?"

Morning Dove began. "Colonel Hazen, Black Kettle is concerned about a few things that he would like to discuss."

"Make it quick. Captain, you can leave now."

Clinton left, but stood outside, just in case there was some verbal conflict or disagreement. He wanted to help these people if he could.

Morning Dove was taken aback by the colonel's unfriendly tone. He was usually friendly to the Indians. Black Kettle spoke in his native tongue and Morning Dove translated. "Colonel, Black Kettle wants to move his 180 lodges near Fort Cobb for protection, as there have been rumours about soldiers coming again."

"No, absolutely not. There is no need. Go back to the Washita where you are camped. The weather is too bad to move now anyway."

There was silence while Morning Dove spoke to Black Kettle. Black Kettle folded his arms and was in deep thought. He responded in his native tongue, Morning Dove translating. "Another request is to go along with the Arapahos to join the camps of the Kiowa and Comanche villages."

"No, of course not. That is a silly idea. Why would you want to do that? You will not be attacked. That is the end of the discussion. Return to your camp. You will be safe there." Colonel Hazen stormed out.

Clinton went back into the stables. He felt sorry for the Indians because no one was helping them or trying to. He told Morning Dove, "Please wait here. I want to make up for the horrible coffee I made. I'll be back soon." Clinton ran to the army trader and bought some baked goods, wrapped them in a cloth napkin from the trader and then ran back to the Indians. Morning Dove, Black Kettle and the others were leading their horses out of the stables.

"Morning Dove, here is some food for your long trip back," Clinton said, handing her the napkin. "You need all the energy you can get. It looks like the weather isn't going to get any better. You can always stay here and travel tomorrow."

"That is very kind of you, Clinton, but Black Kettle wants to return to his people."

"Very well, but if the weather gets worse you can always come back. I am so glad you can speak English. It does make my life easier. Also, I was going to ask before you go if you ever knew or heard of a white captive girl. She had blonde curly hair and her name was Nancy."

"No, Clinton, I know nothing about that. We do not keep White captives, we return them to their people. Thank you for helping us. Black Kettle does appreciate it. He told me so and wishes that all army men were like you."

"Why is that?"

"Because you showed kindness. You weren't scared of us. You showed us respect. We must leave now to make it back to our village before dark." They mounted their horses and left the fort.

The Cheyenne made their journey back home through the ice and snow. Morning Dove pulled her buffalo robe up to her ears to stop her face from freezing. She let her robe drape freely over Prairie Moon's rump to give her horse warmth. It was a silent journey until Morning Dove broke the peace and asked Black Kettle, "Can we trust the word of Chief Hazen? He wasn't very happy today, as if something was troubling him. He seemed nervous."

"He was acting a bit strange. Maybe he was on the firewater. No, I don't think we can trust him, but we do have to obey his orders. If we go against him, we will be in big trouble with the soldiers and the Great Father in Washington — they will not hesitate to create war on the Cheyenne. We do not want that. I suppose we have to stay where we are on the Washita, for the time being."

Morning Dove pondered for a moment. "But, I think we can trust Chief Hazen, surely he wouldn't allow the army to attack us, as we are peaceful and he knows where we are. He can protect us."

"I would rather move away from the Washita as there have been rumours from scouts of a large body of soldiers moving in this direction, but we are stuck where we are and cannot do as we please. The White Man holds us at his mercy. Sooner rather than later all Indian tribes, even our enemies, will face the same fate as us. We have to walk with the White Man on a path of peace."

"You have been so gracious with the Whites, so patient. You are my hero. I look up to you and have learnt so much and am so glad that you wanted me to learn the White Man's tongue. I feel so proud that I can translate and help my tribe. I feel powerful in that role."

"I am glad you feel that way, and the best way to help our tribe is to always be one step ahead of the White Man and try to predict what he will do next. When I pass over to the other side, I know you will be able to help our tribe by being able to talk with the Whites, and you can teach it to your children and to the rest of the tribe. I know that the army interpreters translate things wrong to us. How are we ever going to know what is going on when they lie and mislead us with their words?"

Morning Dove was silent. She didn't know what to say to that question.

The arduous journey brought them back to their village, their winter wonderland. It looked so pretty: the top of the tepees were covered in snow and the glow of fires could be seen coming from the tepees as snow trickled down — the whiteness making it look magical. Morning Dove gently brushed off the snowflakes on top of her head.

"Morning Dove, I am going to organise a council tonight with my fellow chiefs. You must be exhausted, go and get some rest."

"Alright, Father. I will see you in the morning, but I will attend to the horses first."

Black Kettle was waiting in his tepee for his fellow tribesmen to arrive. Once they had all arrived, Black Kettle began speaking. "My fellow men, I have gone to see Chief Hazen. He was very mysterious, it seemed as though he was trying to hide something from us. He will not allow us to move from the Washita or join other camps. You are well aware of the rumours that soldiers are approaching. I feel unsettled that we have to stay here." There was silence while the chiefs took in what was said.

"If there is a chance of attack, we should move, no matter what Chief Hazen says," said Buffalo Star.

"We should organise our warriors in defensive positions so we can be ready for them, or let's find them and attack them first," said Tall Bear.

"If we do find the soldiers, we could always organise a parley and show them we do not want to fight as we are peaceful Indians," said White Feather.

"If we do meet up with them first, a parley is a good idea, and surely the most peaceful way," Black Kettle said. "We cannot have the soldiers attack like they did at Sand Creek. We have to make the first move. It is settled. A group of us will ride out and find the soldiers in the morning."

Everyone nodded in agreement and left to retire to their lodges.

18

Battle of Washita

T he next day, November 27th 1868, Black Kettle woke
early; the birds had started singing and the light of
day had just shown itself. He stepped out of his tepee to
a magical snow blissed dome that made the village look
pure and untouched. Snowflakes were falling, making it
even more blissful. The crisp air filled his lungs with pure
fresh oxygen. Fog gathered on the Washita River, making
it appear very mysterious. He started to walk through the
snow, crunching as he went. A lone woman covered in
her buffalo robe was returning to her tepee after a latrine
stop. As she looked towards the horizon, she yelled, "Soldiers! Soldiers!"

Black Kettle's heart jumped and he surveyed the horizon, spotting movement — he could see horses and
soldiers. He ran to his tepee to grab his gun, yelling, "Soldiers are coming!" He told his sleeping family to get up
before running back outside and firing his gun into the
air. "Get Up! Get Up! Soldiers are coming!"

Chaos and terror filled the village.

Everyone was frantic, not knowing which way to go or

what to do. The attachment of soldiers galloped into the village from four different directions. Black Kettle could see General Custer at the head of the column, leading the seventh cavalry of eight hundred soldiers in all directions through to the village. The soldiers fired shots indiscriminately, hitting anyone who moved.

Medicine Woman Later was encouraging Morning Dove to hurry and get dressed. "You go, Mama. I'll be right behind you."

Medicine Woman Later rushed from the tepee and was caught in the chaos. Morning Dove finished putting her clothes on and went to follow her mother out. She froze when she saw soldiers swarming the village, shooting. They'd shoot her if they saw her running. She stayed in the tepee, hiding under her buffalo robe. She started thinking about Clinton McKay. Surely if he was here he would protect and rescue her. She was scared of what could happen. All she could hear were gunshots, horses' galloping hooves, yelling and screaming. She hid further under her buffalo robe, shaking.

The Indian warriors tried to defend the women and children, using guns and bows and arrows, but the soldier's firepower was so fierce they had to flee for safety. Black Kettle heard his wife yelling his name. She was leading some of his tribespeople. He saw her and grabbed her arm. The soldiers were galloping in and around the village. Black Kettle found a loose cavalry horse and hurled his wife on top and then himself. He saw a few soldiers coming his way and held his hand up in a gesture of peace. Someone fired and a bullet ripped through Black Kettle's stomach and another in his back. He toppled into the snow. The man who put peace and his fellow Southern Cheyenne first, and who did everything in his power to walk by the White Man's requests, lay dead.

More gunshots followed and Medicine Woman Later suffered the same fate as her husband, falling in the snow and grabbing Black Kettle's hand in a final gesture to travel together in the land of forever.

Suddenly there was silence. Morning Dove heard the gunshots stop and was tempted to flee but she couldn't move; her body was frozen in place.

Someone entered her tepee. "Get up! Get up! I know you are hiding under there. Come on, get up." Morning Dove peeked out from under her buffalo robe and saw a blue cavalry hat. "Move. I know you don't understand English but move." He kicked her.

Morning Dove pushed to her feet on shaky legs, pulling the buffalo robe around her, and followed the soldier from the tepee. What she saw made her cry. Countless bodies lay in the pure snow, staining it red. It was Sand Creek all over again.

"You need to walk this way." The soldier shoved her in the back and led Morning Dove to where a circle of captured women, children and elders were gathered.

Morning Dove panicked. She couldn't see Black Kettle or Medicine Woman Later. She wandered away, trying to find them.

"Hey! Get back here. Get back now, squaw." The soldier ran towards her, and dragged her back to the circle.

Terror overwhelmed everyone's eyes. Morning Dove pretended she didn't know English, to keep her one step ahead of what the soldiers were thinking; Black Kettle had taught her well. There were orders to slaughter the horse herd. The soldiers had rounded up the horses and brought them into the centre of the village. Morning Dove saw Prairie Moon, her heart squeezing. Soldiers started shooting the horses, their bodies falling to the icy ground. Prairie Moon became fractious and made a run for it with a group of other horses, escaping into the distance. The shooting continued until all the remaining horses lay dead. The troopers herded the women, children and elderly and made them march to Camp Supply.

Clinton stayed at Fort Cobb longer than he'd wanted to as there were reports of an Indian uprising — bands were on the move after what had happened at the Washita. Clinton was at Colonel Hazen's quarters. "What are you saying, Colonel, that there was a battle at the Washita led by General Custer and Indians have died?"

"Yes, that's right, Captain. General Custer surprised them in the early hours of the morning. It was Black Kettle's village."

"What?! They were just here yesterday, sir. They were peaceful. Don't tell me they were killed."

"The reports are trickling back that Black Kettle was killed. I don't know about the girl. They have captured the women and children and taken them back to Camp Supply."

"I just don't believe it. How could this happen? How can you attack a peaceful village?" Clinton asked, furious.

"Well, if you ask me, good riddance."

"You knew all along that this was going to happen? I overheard what you said to Morning Dove. You forced them to stay at their winter camp. How could you do that? They seemed so determined to have peace. I am glad I was ill and not fit to be in the battle. That is just plain slaughter."

"Why be in the army when you know that you have to fight them? I think you better change careers before it is too late."

Clinton was silent, his face red, embarrassed by what Colonel Hazen said. Maybe he was right, Clinton thought. Clinton knew he had to depart Colonel Hazen's quarters before he said or did something silly, like wrestling him to the floor.

"I'm leaving for Camp Supply now. I have to see if Morning Dove and the other members are okay." Clinton advised.

"The Indians are angry and they won't let you through if they see you, but suit yourself, it's your scalp." Replied Colonel Hazen.

Clinton said, "I will leave in the morning then and make it through. I will make sure of that, and the Indians will start to move away from the area now, so the morning is a good time."

Clinton left Colonel Hazen hoping not to run into him again before he left the fort. He went back to his room, wondering what would have happened if he had been fit enough to fight. There was no way he could have fired at these people. He believed they were living in peace. He would have had to pretend, firing bullets over the Cheyenne's heads. If he had refused to fight, he would have been charged. Clinton counted his blessings that he was ill; it was his saving grace.

Clinton journeyed back to Camp Supply on Ranger, who had been stabled at Fort Cobb while Clinton recovered from his illness. They both paid close attention to any sounds that might alert them to an attack. The icy wind made Clinton shiver; the snow blissed environment looked pure and beautiful. He rested halfway through the journey behind a tree that had cover. His food had frozen and he didn't want to risk the smell of smoke giving away his position to any enemies so he carried on hungry. He found a stream that wasn't frozen over and dipped his tin cup into it, drinking the freezing liquid, shivering even more.

Suddenly, he heard movement in the snow and could see the bobbing of heads with Indian feathers blowing in the breeze. Clinton told Ranger to keep still and quiet. The Indians disappeared down a ravine. It seemed to be three families travelling, most likely to a new camp. Clinton stayed where he was for at least another thirty minutes. He prayed to God to help him make his way back. "Please, God, grant me safe passage back so I can protect Morning Dove, if she survived. Amen."

Clinton was traversing through the snow with Ranger and could see the outline of Camp Supply; he was nearly there. "Thank you, God," he said quietly. Once he got there, he stormed into Custer's headquarters, finding him penning a letter.

"Captain McKay, what can I do for you?" General Custer flipped the letter over, hiding its contents from Clinton.

"General Custer, I have just returned from Fort Cobb." Clinton paused for a moment, trying to catch his breath.

"Yes, I can see that, Captain McKay."

"I heard about the Battle of Washita, sir. I am disgusted with what happened. I saw Black Kettle with other tribe members at Fort Cobb just the other day. They went to Colonel Hazen to ask permission to relocate. He refused because he knew about the War Department's plan and wanted them killed. They were peaceful Indians. They were not hostiles."

"Captain McKay, settle down. You were not at the battle so I suggest you keep your opinion to yourself. I am still your general. I can easily have you up on charges for speaking to me so brazenly. My orders were to control the hostile situation."

"There was no hostile situation to control, General. They were innocent. It was wrong."

"Do not question my orders or motives ever again. You have only just arrived here. I suggest you leave your nose out of my business."

Clinton stormed out. He had to find Morning Dove as soon as possible — if she was alive. They were being held temporarily at the back of the camp in an area patrolled by cavalry. He searched where the captives were, but couldn't find her. Then, as he was leaving, a woman came out of a makeshift tent. It was her.

Clinton's heart skipped a beat. "Morning Dove, do you remember me? I saw you at the fort. My name is Clinton."

"Yes, I remember."

"My condolences for the loss of your father and mother. I am truly sorry. It should not have happened. I had no involvement in it."

Morning Dove looked at Clinton, but couldn't bring herself to say anything. She was thinking of Black Kettle and Medicine Woman Later. For the first time in her life she felt completely alone.

"Morning Dove, I am really sorry. It was an absolute tragedy. If you need anything, please find me."

The next day, Clinton headed for the Cheyenne's camp and found Morning Dove playing with a handful of children, trying to make them smile. Once she saw Clinton she sent them on their way.

"Morning Dove, I have found some extra blankets for you and your people. There are not many, but it will help during the night. I know the makeshift tents aren't that warm, especially this time of year. I'll be back. I will obtain some food for your people. I think I have some flour, sugar, coffee and dried beef to spare."

Clinton returned with the supplies and gave them to Morning Dove, who was talking to some women huddled in a circle, trying to keep each other warm. "Excuse me,

Morning Dove. Here are some supplies for you and your people. I literally had to beg for them."

"Thank you." Morning Dove took them. "Why are you being so kind to us?"

"I feel terrible about what happened. I want to help you and try and make things better."

"I am afraid that a few supplies and blankets won't make things better. We are prisoners of the White Man and have lost our families."

"Please let me help. I cannot undo what has happened, but you must realise I had no part in it. I don't want to upset you. I will leave you alone."

Morning Dove watched Clinton go and that night, while she lay huddled among sleeping Indians in a makeshift tent, freezing, she couldn't help but think of him. *Why am I thinking of this White Man?* As devastated as she was, he kept creeping into her thoughts; somehow, he gave her hope to keep going.

19

Grandmother's Intervention

C linton had lain awake in his tent all night, tossing and turning. His mind had been thinking of everything that had happened since he joined the seventh cavalry. He couldn't work out why Morning Dove was occupying his thoughts more than anything else, and why he wanted to help her so much. He'd go looking for her this morning, just to see her. Clinton dressed himself and found his bible and dime novel, thinking Morning Dove would like them.

Clinton walked into the middle of the Cheyenne's camp and found Morning Dove organising food for the women and children. "Good morning, Morning Dove. I brought you a couple of things that I thought you might like, seeing that you are stuck here for a while. Knowing that you can read and speak English, here is my bible. I know we have two different gods, but you might find it interesting. And here's a dime novel about the Wild West. You can keep them for as long as you need."

"You don't need to give me gifts. I don't know if I should accept them. I shouldn't be having contact with you."

"Let's just say the books are on loan, and of course you can have contact with me."

"But you are my captor. It wouldn't be right to talk to you casually. We must keep a formal distance. I also don't want the soldiers or General Custer knowing I can speak English."

"I won't tell them. You have my word on that, and I want to get to know you. I didn't capture you so I'm not your captor. If anything, I would have rescued you if I was there."

Morning Dove stared into Clinton's eyes, dumbfounded someone could be so friendly and kind. She couldn't say anything but she felt cared for and remembered the morning of the battle when she'd wished for Clinton to save her.

"I have to attend to the horses now, but I will see you later on."

"Clinton, I don't think it is a good idea. People are looking at us already, especially some of the soldiers over there. They know we have become friendly and talk to each other. It is better we keep our distance. I don't want any trouble."

"It's okay, Morning Dove, and don't worry about the soldiers. I can handle them. I don't think there is anything wrong with talking as long as they don't hear us. We are allowed to communicate. Alright, I will give you some space. I am leaving this morning to go on a search party. Goodbye."

Morning Dove stared at Clinton as he left. Why was she pushing him away? She felt she needed to, but now regretted her decision. She just wanted to run to him.

Camp Supply was organising a search party for Major Elliot and his eighteen men, who had disappeared at the battle of the Washita. Major Elliot and his men were last seen charging up a trail to capture any Indians who had escaped. They were never seen again. Clinton was going with General Custer, General Sherman, who was visiting, Tom and a detachment of soldiers. They were mounted on their horses, organising their formation, with General Custer at the lead. Clinton dipped his hat to Morning Dove as he rode by. Unbeknown to Clinton, it made Morning Dove's heart leap. Clinton felt alive as he trudged through the thick snow on horseback thinking of Morning Dove; she inspired him.

The attachment of soldiers were careful as they made their way through the territory, well aware that a horde of angry Indians could attack at any time. They managed to make it to the Washita battle site without incident.

Clinton was horrified by what he saw: burnt remains of the village and dead bodies. Flocks of ravens and crows, too many to count, watched the soldiers. Wolves were gnawing on bodies and growled as the troopers came closer. The flocks of birds flew into the sky as the command made its way forward, darkening the sky like a black shadow. The wolves soon fled as well.

Clinton felt sick to the stomach and couldn't look at the site any longer. The soldiers followed a trail across a small outcrop of the Washita River.

Tom looked down from a steep bank. "There's something down there. It looks like a body," Tom told his brother.

"We need to continue on and follow the rest of the trail," General Custer commanded.

Soon they found what they were looking for: Major Elliot's men dead, all gathered in a circle, disfigured and mutilated. Everyone dismounted and assessed what had happened. Clinton stared at the men and had to walk away, feeling as though he would vomit. There was silence among the men while they took to the gruesome task of burying their comrades.

They thought they had finished burying their men when they came across a lone body some distance away from the others. Clinton bent down to examine the body. "It seems to me this man may have been taken alive, but there is a close range bullet hole in his skull that could indicate he killed himself."

The men stared at Clinton, not really knowing what to say. It scared them. They finished burying the last fallen soldier and travelled back to Camp Supply in silence, an air of gloom descending over the troop. It was late in the afternoon when the cavalry attachment returned to the camp with sad, stunned faces. Clinton detached from the others when he spotted Morning Dove at her camp's perimeter with a book in her hand. He dismounted Ranger and tied him to a post before heading to the Cheyenne camp where he told the three soldiers on duty what had happened. He asked them to give the others a hand with the horses, so he would have an opportunity to talk to Morning Dove without anyone watching.

Morning Dove approached Clinton, holding out his

bible. "I wanted to give this back to you. I just don't understand it. It seems too complicated. I have started reading the other novel. I am enjoying it. Are you okay? You seem a bit upset."

"I'm alright. It is good to see you," said Clinton as he put the bible in his back pocket.

"Talking may be too risky with soldiers around. They might hear my English tongue," Morning Dove whispered.

"There is no one here now. They are attending the horses and then it will be time for supper. I am the watch guard until the others get back. How are you feeling? Are you alright?"

"It is hard to know how I am feeling. There has been a terrible and unjust tragedy to my people. I miss Black Kettle and Medicine Woman Later, they adopted me after my original parents were killed by a White Man's disease, and I do not know where my brother Black Beaver is. He went off with the dog soldiers so I don't know if he is alive. I have my adopted grandmother, but she is very frail now. The whole tribe looks after her and the other elders. I may not have any family left." Morning Dove sighed. "Where is your family, Clinton?"

"I only have my sister, Charlotte, and her two daughters, Grace and Barbara. I haven't seen them for about two years. We do correspond regularly, and my nieces send me painted pictures and drawings. The latest news is that Charlotte has remarried. That is all I know, apart from my new brother-in-law's name being Mathew. Charlotte never gave me any other details. I hope she is doing well.

She deserves happiness. I really do miss them and feel guilty that I am not there."

Morning Dove turned around and couldn't believe her eyes. She saw horses around the outside of the camp. "Clinton, look. See over there? That is my horse Prairie Moon, and a couple of our Indian horses. They escaped the onslaught. Can we get them?"

"They are outside the camp's perimeters. Will they be easy to catch?"

"Yes, they will be as they know me. I need a couple of rope halters. Will the general let me keep them?"

"I don't see why not. I will come with you. You can catch them and I will bring them back here. But be quick because I really shouldn't let you wander from the perimeters. Just wait here and I will grab some ropes."

Clinton returned with a couple of ropes and very cautiously let Morning Dove roam out of the camp's perimeters. Morning Dove approached the horses. Prairie Moon whinnied and trotted towards her, the others following. Morning Dove gave her horse a big hug, not wanting to let her go. She placed the rope halter over her head and managed to catch one of the other horses, which was pure black with a white blaze. She handed both halters to Clinton while she went over to the spotted horse.

"Clinton, hold them steady," Morning Dove warned as both horses were rearing up and Clinton had to be careful of their hooves coming down. Morning Dove quickly gathered the last horse and took Prairie Moon off Clinton's hands. "Where can we put them?"

"Look. The three guards are coming back. Quick, give me the horses. Get back into camp," said Clinton in a hurry.

Clinton took all three horses, which settled down now that they were together. He spoke to the three guards. "Found some Indian horses on the outskirts. I will put them in the corral — the one next to the picket line and then see General Custer for permission to keep them."

The three guards nodded and left to return to their patrol of the Cheyenne camp, not seeming interested.

Clinton noticed General Custer sitting outside his tent on an old wooden chair, engrossed in his letter writing. "Excuse me, General, sorry to disturb you."

"What is it, Captain McKay?"

"Sir, I found three Indian horses on the camp's outskirts. They are in the corral at the moment. They are decent types. With your permission, sir, can I keep them as my own, or offer them into the US cavalry?"

"We do not have any use for Indian horses in the US Cavalry. Do you really want to be responsible for them?"

"I just thought of an idea, sir. The captives could keep them or we could give them to Indian scouts — apart from the buckskin, which belongs to one of the Indian women."

"I am not concerned about the horses. I have more important things to attend to."

"What about the buckskin, sir? Can the Indian woman keep her?"

"Why are you so concerned about this buckskin?"

Clinton was silent for a moment, before he responded, "It's a nice horse and the woman is devoted to it, sir."

"Very well, she can keep it. It's your responsibility to take care of them until it's time to leave Camp Supply, and then I will work out what to do. Is that all, Captain?"

"Yes, thank you, sir."

After supper, in the cover of darkness, Clinton went back to inform Morning Dove about the horses. Most of the soldiers were in their tents, playing cards or getting an early night's sleep. Clinton walked towards the Cheyenne camp to find Morning Dove; he spotted her sitting outside of her tent, watching the night sky.

Clinton needed a way to get rid of the patrol guards so he could speak to Morning Dove. He called the guards over and said, "You can all be relieved of your posts and grab some hot coffee. It's freezing out here. I'll keep watch until you get back." They were very grateful and headed off. He was lucky the guards were different to the last time; otherwise they may have become suspicious.

Clinton waved Morning Dove over to the edge of the perimeter. "Morning Dove, you can keep Prairie Moon," he said once they were out of sight.

Morning Dove was ecstatic and without thinking hugged Clinton. She pulled away quickly, afraid that someone might see their embrace. They both looked at each other, bewildered. They felt feelings inside their hearts, but were unsure what they were.

Morning Dove quickly came back to reality and said,

"Thank you, Clinton. I cannot believe General Custer allowed me to keep Prairie Moon."

"I used my charm, that's all." He grinned. "The other two might be given to Indian scouts or your tribe — the general isn't sure yet. How would you like helping me care for them?"

"I would love to. Thank you, Clinton, for convincing General Custer to keep them. I am so happy that my best friend is back with me," Morning Dove said excitedly.

"I am glad you are happy. You deserve to be happy, Morning Dove, and if there is anything else I can do for you, please ask."

"Why are you being so kind to me? No White Man is ever kind to an Indian, unless they have a reason for it."

"I do not have an ulterior motive. I just want to help you. I am not like the typical white men you come across. Just give me a chance to prove myself."

Morning Dove nodded, believing what he said. There was laughter from a distance; the guards were coming back to their post.

"Morning Dove, you better go back to your tent so they don't see you."

She stared into Clinton's eyes for a moment before going. The guards approached and Clinton left to retire to his tent.

Morning Dove awoke after a restless night of thinking about Clinton and what an amazing man he was. She didn't want to wake up; she wanted to keep dreaming about Clinton. She heard voices outside, the snorting of horses, clinking of bridles and the bugler calls. It was time to rise. She yawned and stretched her body out, still feeling tired.

She decided a brisk walk in the fresh winter air would liven her up and made her way outside. She walked quickly around the camp. Her stomach felt as if it were in knots. She was driving herself crazy with sensual thoughts about Clinton. Every time she thought of him her stomach hurt. Her nerves were getting the better of her. *Why do I feel this way?*

She decided to see her adopted grandmother, Runs With Horses, who was housed in the same tent as her. Even though Runs With Horses was frail, her mind was sharp. Morning Dove entered the tent. Runs With Horses was eating some of her hidden pemmican. She smiled. "My sweet granddaughter, I can see your heart is heavy with trouble. Your mind is not centred with the Great Spirit. Your head is saying one thing and your heart another."

"Oh, Runs With Horses, I am troubled."

"Come, child, lie down." Runs With Horses opened up a small pouch, filled with dried herbs. She mixed the herbs carefully and placed them in a carved stone, which she had secretly stored. She started burning the herbs and an aromatic smell flooded the tent. She held the stone upwards, towards the sky, and started chanting before bringing the carved stone to the right and then the left. She sprinkled the herbs on the earth of the tent. "Breathe, Morning Dove, breathe. Close your eyes and let the spirits talk."

Morning Dove tried to relax and let the Great Spirit give her advice. She could see Clinton's face in her mind. He was laughing and calling her name. Why was the Great Spirit showing her Clinton? *What does this mean?* She pondered and dreamed of him even more. Suddenly, with a shudder, she opened her eyes.

"The Great Spirit must have given you an answer," Runs With Horses said. "Follow the Great Spirit's advice and hold it deep in your heart."

Morning Dove felt dazed about what she'd seen. *What does this mean? Does it mean Clinton is my future and to hold him close to my heart like Grandmother said? That can't be right. A Cheyenne with a cavalry officer... we would be the laughing stock of the entire country. The meaning from the Great Spirit must be interpreted in a different way as Clinton and I couldn't possibly be together.* Morning Dove thanked her grandmother and left.

Clinton was carrying army supply rations into the Cheyenne camp with a few other soldiers. He'd volunteered for this duty, hoping he might see Morning Dove. The Cheyenne gathered around the soldiers in anticipation of the delivery. There was noisy chatter amongst them. Clinton spotted Morning Dove but she pretended not to see him and walked away. He followed her while the other soldiers were busy rationing supplies out.

"Morning Dove, wait."

"Hello, Captain, I must hurry."

"Why do you need to hurry?"

"I have important things to do."

"Like what? I could help."

"It is not your concern. You shouldn't talk to me all the time, or keep checking on me. I can take care of myself. I am sure you have other things to do, being a captain and all. I think we need to give each other some space. We have been spending too much time together."

"Morning Dove, look at me. What's going on? You have never spoken to me like that. Someone has said something about us, haven't they?"

"There is no us, and never will be. It's not right."

"Who has the right to say that?"

"I do. I have to look after my tribe."

"Your tribe will be fine. They are very resourceful people. Do you want to tell me what is wrong?"

"I really have to go."

Clinton put both his hands on her shoulders. "Morning Dove, I don't know what has happened, but I like spending time with you. I will continue to do so no matter what people say. I feel alive when I am with you. Don't shut me out. We need each other," Clinton pleaded.

"I can't think. We need to keep our distance from each other. I need space."

"Space for what? Did someone say something?"

"Look at us, Clinton. We are on different sides here. I am Cheyenne, you are in the cavalry. It just can't work. People will cause us misery if we're together — not that we are together. I will have to go to a reservation shortly. I am not free, but you have your freedom."

"Hang on, what are you trying to say? That you want us to be together? Do you have feelings for me?"

Morning Dove didn't know what to say.

"Tell me the truth, Morning Dove. How do you really feel? Please tell me, no more games."

"Clinton, my heart aches. I can't think. I can't eat. My stomach is in knots. I don't know how all this happened. I have developed feelings for you. I just can't understand it. I don't know what to do about these forbidden feelings."

"Are you in love with me?" Clinton asked, hoping for the right answer.

"Yes, Clinton. You make me feel whole, but we can't be in love. It shouldn't have happened," Morning Dove said in tears.

"I can't believe you said that you love me. Tell me again."

"I love you, Clinton."

"Well, that is a relief."

"Why do you say that?"

"I feel the same way. I love you, Morning Dove. I don't know how these feelings developed either, but they have. We can't ignore them any longer."

"Clinton, why do you love me? It would be easier if you didn't."

"I love you because you are strong. There is something different and special about you. You are graceful in everything you do. You are beautiful and show so much love for your tribe. You are wonderful and my life wouldn't be the same if you weren't in it. Can I ask you the same question? Why do you love me?"

"You are kind, warm and have looked after me so well. You're special and I love the way you make me feel when I am near you. You make me feel safe and at peace. I don't know what to do."

"It will be alright," said Clinton. He whispered, "It will be okay. We will work something out, as long as I know you want to be with me and you love me, that is all that matters."

"I do, Clinton, I do. But…"

"No, there are no 'but's'. Don't ever doubt what we have between us. It's special. Yes, the circumstances we are in are tricky, but where there is a will there is a way. I have to go now and help with rationing the supplies. Those Cheyenne of yours are very noisy, but that's good because no one would have heard us. Meet me at the back of the camp near the big elm tree tonight, after supper. Be careful." Morning Dove nodded. "I love you, Morning Dove." He left to return to his duties.

Morning Dove pressed her hand to her heart, afraid it might explode. *Maybe the Great Spirit is right. Maybe there is a future with Clinton… but how?*

Morning Dove quietly made her way to the old elm tree, careful not to arouse the guards' suspicions. It was dark enough for her to go unnoticed, but there was a trickle of moonlight that helped her see where she was going. She could see a shape nearby and hoped it was Clinton. She realised she was wrong when a faint smell of cigarette smoke drifted towards her. It was a lieutenant she didn't like — the one with the evil eyes. She hid behind one of the tents. She waited for him to leave, feeling as though an eternity passed before he finally moved on.

Morning Dove hurried to the elm tree and hid behind it. Someone approached her from behind and she knew instinctively it was Clinton. He put his arms around her waist and she felt a sudden jolt of passion. Clinton touched Morning Dove's cheek and brushed it with his fingertips softly, then his fingers moved to her lips and traced their outline.

Morning Dove stood motionless, anticipating what was going to happen next. She was waiting to feel his sweet lips on hers. Their kiss was gentle at first, but became more passionate, and before Morning Dove knew it she was wrapped in Clinton's arms, entranced. She quickly broke away, breathless.

"Clinton, this is wrong. What would people say? We can't do this. We have to stop now."

"Morning Dove, it will be alright. People don't matter. We want to be with each other. My life won't be the same without you in it. Stop running away from me." Clinton moved closer and whispered, "We are not running anymore."

Morning Dove's body was aching with desire for Clinton. Clinton moved in and placed his hands on her cheeks and pulled her towards him, kissing her more passionately than the first time. Their bodies seemed to fuse together, becoming one. The kiss seemed to last an eternity, their passion never ending.

Clinton broke from the kiss and smiled at Morning

Dove, mesmerised by her beauty. He touched her cheek and her lips gently, and ran his fingers down her long black silken hair. "You are so beautiful, especially in the moonlight. I love you, Morning Dove."

"I love you, Clinton."

They fell into passion's embrace once more. Suddenly, they heard voices coming towards them. They hid behind the tree and prayed no one would see them. Five cavalry lieutenants walked in a crooked line, singing drunkenly. They did not know where they were going, tripping over themselves and laughing hysterically as they did so, but somehow they made it back to their tents.

Clinton and Morning Dove sighed in relief.

"That was close," Clinton said. "We need to keep our love a secret until things settle down, and see each other when we can. Don't ever doubt our love. I hope to figure out what to do."

"So we will just have to sneak around, hiding our feelings?" Morning Dove asked, concerned. "I don't want to hide and sneak around."

Clinton nodded. "We do need to be careful when we meet with each other. I just have to figure out what to do."

"Now I am scared because of our situation."

"Don't be scared, Morning Dove, we will work it out. We should go back now. You go first and I will wait a couple of minutes then follow."

Morning Dove nodded and left Clinton by the tree.

Clinton couldn't sleep all night, tossing and turning.

His mind was working overtime. What could he do? He couldn't think of a way out. He was struggling to find a solution. He couldn't sneak around with Morning Dove forever. It wouldn't be fair to Morning Dove or himself.

The next morning, two lieutenants approached Morning Dove, who was chatting to some of the Indian women outside her tent. "Hey, squaw. General Custer wants to see you. He knows you speak English. Looks like we've got an English speaking squaw here, what a novelty."

"Come on, Joseph, don't be too hard on the lady. Oops, I mean squaw. Can you read as well? Maybe you can read us a bedtime story. Joseph and I get mighty lonely at night."

"Let's go, Eddie, General Custer will be counting down the minutes until we get back."

Morning Dove was in shock, not sure how anyone could know she spoke English. She dreaded seeing Custer. She felt knots and twists in her stomach. The two lieutenants walked behind her, laughing all the way. Morning Dove wanted to throw something at them, like a large stone that would knock them unconscious for a few days.

They entered the officers' tent where they found General Custer writing a letter. "General Custer, Morning Dove is here," Eddie announced.

"Very well, you're dismissed." General Custer placed his pen down.

How do they know my name? Morning Dove asked herself.

"Good morning, Morning Dove. I am General Custer. Someone reported that you can speak English and I wanted to talk to you about being a translator for your people. I am afraid the Cheyenne way of life is coming to an end. Eventually all the tribes will be rounded up, and the future lies within the White Man's ways. Come now and have some breakfast."

Morning Dove sat hesitantly on a squeaky chair that felt very uncomfortable. Her head was still spinning with uncertainty and she couldn't speak just yet.

"Here is a plate of biscuits, gravy with bacon and hot coffee." He pushed a plate in front of her. "I know you aren't accustomed to these foods but they are delicious."

Morning Dove was uncertain what the food would taste like. She tried the strong coffee, but nearly spat it out. She finally succumbed to the hot biscuits, bacon and gravy. She scoffed them down. She hadn't eaten properly for a while.

General Custer jokingly said, "Slow down, girl, remember to breathe."

Morning Dove gulped down the last of the food. "General, how did you know my name and that I spoke English?"

"Someone heard you while you were talking to Captain McKay. Your people trust you and we need you to be an interpreter. Don't be afraid. It is quite simple. You relay to your people what we need to tell them."

"What if I don't want to?"

"I am afraid that is not an option. There is nothing to it. Either you want to help your people and have plenty of rations or you want them to starve."

There was no other option. Morning Dove nodded in agreement and left, accompanied by the two lieutenants who had been waiting outside.

Clinton saw this and intervened. "Lieutenants, you are excused. I will escort her back."

The lieutenants turned away and started laughing. Clinton began walking with Morning Dove, who whispered, "They know I can speak English. General Custer wanted to see me about being an interpreter. Someone overheard us talking."

Clinton was silent for a moment, not knowing what to say. "I am sorry, Morning Dove. I know you didn't want them to find out."

"I knew this would happen. It puts me in awkward position. If they tell me things that aren't true, or are not going to happen, and I have to relay that to the tribe, I will be stuck in the middle and they will make me look bad."

"I suppose in some way you can use it to your advantage. You have control in what is being said to your tribe. Just filter out what you need to if you don't trust the words of whoever is speaking."

"Thanks, Clinton, maybe I do have power after all."

20

Dog Soldiers

T he next day, Clinton walked past the Cheyenne camp to see if he could catch a glimpse of Morning Dove. He noticed a lieutenant harassing her. He was calling her names and pulling her hair in a gesture of scalping. Clinton ran over to protect her. "Lieutenant, I think it is best you move on and leave the lady alone. I think she deserves an apology, don't you?"

"But, Captain, it was just a bit of fun, no harm in it."

"Lieutenant, I don't want you in arm's length of Morning Dove, and that's an order," Clinton said assertively. "Where's the apology?"

The lieutenant looked at Morning Dove. "Sorry," he said quickly.

"I think she deserves more of an apology than that."

"I'm sorry, ma'am, it will never happen again."

"Off you go now, and I don't want you near this lady again. Do I make myself clear?"

"Yes, Captain," the lieutenant said, moving away quickly.

"Are you okay, Morning Dove? He didn't hurt you, did he?" a concerned Clinton asked.

"No, I'm fine. Thank you, Captain, but I can look after myself."

"I don't doubt you can, but the army contains unsavoury characters that could harm you. My advice is to never be alone with any one of them."

"Does that include you as well?"

"No, I'm not talking about me. I would never hurt you. I want to protect you," Clinton said, looking straight into Morning Dove's eyes. "I'm just saying be careful."

"Yes, Captain." Morning Dove turned to walk away.

"Wait, I have to deliver dispatches to Fort Lyon. Would you like to come and see your precious land? I will have to get permission to take you."

"I would like that. Can I take Prairie Moon?"

"I don't see why not. Stay here. I am going to see the general." Clinton hurried off to find General Custer, feeling excited. He hoped Morning Dove would be allowed to accompany him. Clinton walked towards General Custer's tent but noticed him near the picket line, inspecting the horses. "Excuse me, General." General Custer turned from the horse he was examining. "General, sir, I am going to take the dispatches to Captain Taylor at Fort Lyon. I would like to take one of the Cheyenne captives with me."

"Why do you want to take a captive with you?"

"Well, General, if I have any trouble on the frontier, she can speak English and Cheyenne — and also knows Indian sign language."

"Morning Dove is the one you want to take?"

"Yes, sir."

"I don't think you need an Indian squaw for protection. Are you scared of what's out there?"

"I'm not scared, sir. I have fought Indians before. It's just a precaution."

"Very well," the general replied, not wanting to spend any more time on the subject.

"Much, obliged, General."

"Captain, these are the dispatches." He reached into his jacket pocket. "I expect you to be back before sundown."

"Yes, sir," Clinton said excitedly. He raced back to Morning Dove, smiling, feeling very proud of himself. She was waiting where he'd left her. Clinton ushered her over. "Morning Dove, are you ready to go?"

"I can go?"

"Yes, but we must be back before sundown, which will just give us enough time to get to the fort, rest the horses and then come back — unless something happens on the way."

They both went to the horse corral and as they walked passed a group of soldiers, they could hear sneering and laughter. Clinton ignored them. He couldn't make out exactly what they were saying, but he assumed they had noticed all the time he spent with Morning Dove.

Morning Dove and Clinton made it to the corral where Prairie Moon was. Morning Dove was excited to see her best friend. She noticed Prairie Moon seemed to be short in her stride as she walked towards Morning Dove. She called out to Clinton who was saddling Ranger. "Prairie Moon is not well. She is having trouble walking."

Clinton made his way towards the horse and had a look at the off foreleg. He held it up and pressed all around the frog area of the hoof. It seemed all clear until he pressed further down and Prairie Moon gave out a whine. Clinton looked at the spot more closely and could see an abscess developing.

"I have found the problem. She has an abscess that needs to be drained and dressed. I need to take her to the vet."

"An abscess? What is that? I have never heard that word before. We must call it something different."

"An abscess is like a sore that contains a white substance called pus. The vet will take good care of her. Just wait here and I will be back shortly."

Clinton made his way to the left of the horse corral where Doctor Fitzpatrick was situated. Clinton called for him at his tent. A moment later, the flap opened and the vet came out. "What can I do for you, Captain?"

"Doctor Fitzpatrick, an Indian pony has an abscess on the off foreleg."

"I'll come and take a look."

Clinton led the way and grabbed a halter as he walked passed the other horses. They entered the corral where Morning Dove was patting her horse. Clinton warned Doctor Fitzpatrick, "She might become a bit skittish as she is not used to white men handling her, as you can see." Prairie Moon was kicking up her back legs in protest of the men coming towards her. "Take good care of her. She belongs to someone special."

"Yes, Captain, I will do my best. I may have to get someone else to help me. She is pretty flighty."

"Just whisper sweet things in her ears, that always calms the ladies down," Clinton said jokingly.

"Maybe that works in your case. I remember back in Texas in my early cowboy days, I whispered sweet words to a lady and she turned around and punched me in the eye. I was talking to the wrong woman — she was someone's wife and the lady I was with had stepped outside. Of course, I was drunk at the time, and when my woman came back in she saw me holding my eye and asked me what had happened. The other lady explained to her what I had said and then my woman slapped me across the cheek. From that day on I never saw either woman again — and never stepped in that dining hall again either. Women! No wonder I have never married. I would rather be in the army and look after the horses."

Clinton laughed. "That's hilarious. Maybe don't whisper anything to Prairie Moon or she might kick you." Clinton chuckled again. "I will see you later, Doc. I have to deliver dispatches."

"Alright, Captain, be careful out there."

Clinton scanned the corral for a horse Morning Dove could ride. There was still a couple of Indian horses that looked in reasonable condition. He didn't want to give her one of the cavalry horses, in case it become fractious with her. There was an Indian horse next to Morning Dove that looked healthy. "Hey, Morning Dove, what about that one? It looks pretty decent."

"Yes, that should be okay."

"Here you go." He handed her the rope halter. "I will let you catch it as it probably won't like me."

Morning Dove captured the horse with ease and led it from the corral. Clinton was transfixed on Morning Dove. He was in awe of her grace, confidence and beauty, but there was something different about her, something that he had never seen in any other woman before. *She's special*, Clinton thought to himself. Morning Dove turned around and saw Clinton staring.

He looked away and said sheepishly, "Okay, I will get my horse." He walked to the picket line where Ranger was. He made sure the girth was tight and placed the bridle over his head before mounting and trotting up to Morning Dove, who was already mounted, riding bareback. Ranger began neighing, indicating he wasn't sure why he was with the Indian horse.

Clinton and Morning Dove made their way through Camp Supply. Clinton noticed many soldiers staring, and snickering about them. It made him feel uneasy but he couldn't think of that now. He had to deliver the dispatches and look after Morning Dove.

They left the camp and trotted towards the rolling hills, where they stopped to survey the landscape. Clinton took out his telescope and looked across the prairie. "It looks all clear, Morning Dove." Morning Dove smiled at him. "Let's pick it up," Clinton said, spurring Ranger into a canter.

As they approached a grove of trees, they pulled their horses up and gave them a breather. "How does it feel to be out in the wilderness and free again, Morning Dove?"

"It makes my heart happy and sad."

"Why two feelings?"

"I'm happy because I'm free riding, with the wind in my hair and roaming through my precious country, and I'm sad because I'm not really free. Soon I will have to live on a reservation."

"I understand what you mean. After the Civil War I was free, but I didn't feel that way. I was trapped by the memories of all I'd endured. I knew the only way to survive was to make peace with those memories and live for the men who didn't make it. I had to move forward and adjust to my new life, or drink my sorrows with whiskey and become a drunkard. What kind of a life is that? That is just a waste. God spared me for a reason."

"The whiskey — fire water — is very bad," Morning Dove said in disgust.

"Unfortunately, things change, Morning Dove, and you have to go with change."

"But, Clinton, this is not change but the destruction of the Cheyenne. We don't have a choice. The White Man comes along and says you have to live like a White Man and farm, as we are going to rob you of your land and put you on a reservation where there is no fresh breeze, no wild game, and no mountain air and we will leave you to perish from disease and starvation. That is not change. That is wrong. To take us away from our precious land and our freedom, our hearts grow heavy with sadness. There are some Indian bands still out there that run free. Why can't you leave them be? I was unlucky to have been captured."

"In one way, I am glad you were captured, because I wouldn't have met you otherwise. I am sorry about what is happening to your tribe. I see things differently and respect the Cheyenne. If I were a Cheyenne, I think it would be better to die free on your own terms, fighting for what you believe in."

"There has been much blood spilt on both sides."

"Yes, there has. I don't know when it will stop. At least you will be safe once you are on the reservation. No one can attack you anymore. Hopefully one day you can go home and things may settle down. The most important thing is your safety."

"Safety?! Black Kettle thought he was safe. He was at peace with the army, but you came and killed him anyway."

Ranger suddenly became fractious. "What is it, boy? I think there is something or someone approaching. Let's take cover in these trees here." They hid with their horses in thick brush. Ranger was acting skittish. "Ranger, keep it down," Clinton whispered.

Clinton knew something was out there, but what? His heart was beating fast. He could hear his heart thumping in his chest in anticipation. Clinton looked towards Morning Dove; they could both hear something approaching. They kept still and silent, waiting, still mounted on their horses.

Suddenly, Indian horses came into view; it was Cheyenne dog soldiers. There was a leader at the front on a pinto pony. He looked strong and muscular, with long midnight hair that shone. He was dressed in buckskin leggings and a blue cavalry jacket, the gold buttons reflecting the sunlight. His face was half painted black, with a white lightning bolt on his left cheek. He had a mean expression on his face.

Clinton felt sick when he saw the cavalry jacket. *Where did he get it? Whose unfortunate soul did it belong to?* This was the type of warrior you didn't want to meet. There were eight more warriors who followed on their ponies. All of the warriors had their faces painted, and were wearing traditional Indian garb. Someone was wearing a US cavalry cap and another was wearing a cavalry jacket.

The dog soldiers stopped directly in front of where they were hiding; they seemed to sense someone was there and kept a sharp eye on their surroundings. They spoke in their native tongue and Morning Dove tried to hear them, but couldn't make out what they were saying. Clinton was really uneasy, but couldn't get his gun ready as they might hear. It seemed like an eternity, just sitting and praying that the Indians didn't find them.

All of a sudden, they galloped away and Clinton sighed in relief. He and Morning Dove stayed where they were for a little while, to make sure the Indians had gone from the area.

"Clinton, they were Cheyenne dog soldiers. I couldn't give away our position as I don't know what they would have done to you. I couldn't risk your life," Morning Dove said with a heavy heart.

"I am sorry, Morning Dove, and thank you for thinking of me. We should continue on to the fort." They made their way out of hiding and were both feeling nervous

about what may happen, but they needed to continue —
there were still a few more hours of riding to go.

They trotted their horses down a steep embankment
and kept themselves in the open, away from trees and
bushes in case someone was waiting to ambush them.

"Are you worried about the rogue bands around? I can
see it in your face," Morning Dove asked.

"Any white man would be worried crossing through
this territory. Ranger lets me know of approaching Indians. He must be able to smell them or something."

"Clinton, you don't have to be worried. I'll look after
you."

"Shouldn't it be the other way around?"

"Well, not in this case. I know how to handle Indians,
especially my people. If you didn't have me here your
scalp might be hanging from a lance."

"You really know how to make a man feel confident —
now I feel really uneasy."

Morning Dove smiled. "Like I said, I'll look after you."
She nudged her horse into a canter.

Clinton yelled, "Wait for me." He didn't want to fall
behind.

Clinton caught up to Morning Dove and they made it
up the steep embankment. Ranger began acting strangely
again, flicking his ears back and prancing.

"Morning Dove, something has upset Ranger again.
There are Indians about somewhere, but where?" They
stopped their horses, but Ranger did not want to stay in
this spot. He was spooked and wanted to gallop. "I have

to let him go. He is too strong for me to hold on to any longer." Ranger fell in to a gallop and Morning Dove's horse did the same, galloping across the prairie.

Suddenly, there was a whoop and dog soldiers rode out from the distant horizon. Morning Dove and Clinton urged their horses on, but the Indians were gaining on them. They could hear the sound of hooves beating down, getting closer and closer.

"Clinton, keep going. Make it over to the bluff. I am turning around to stop this. They are going to run us down," Morning Dove said out of breath.

"Are you sure?"

"There is no time. I have to stop this. Make it towards those bluffs."

Morning Dove turned her horse around and saw the dog soldiers swiftly galloping. Morning Dove waved her hands furiously so they would stop, and to her amazement they did. Now she had to save herself and the man she loved. "I am Morning Dove, a Southern Cheyenne from Black Kettle's tribe. Please don't hurt us. We are just passing through."

A dog soldier stepped off his horse. "Morning Dove, is that you? It's Black Beaver."

Morning Dove jumped from her horse and embraced her brother. "I can't believe you're alive. I know Black Kettle and Medicine Woman Later were killed. I can't believe you survived," said an emotional Black Beaver.

"Oh, Black Beaver, my heart is so grateful that our paths have crossed, and the biggest blessing is that you are alive.

How I have longed for you to be with me through this difficult time. I am a captive at Camp Supply."

"Who was with you?" Black Beaver asked curiously.

"He is my friend. His name is Captain Clinton McKay. Please don't hurt him. He is a friend of the Cheyenne and has been helping me. We were going to Fort Lyon."

"What for? And why were you going? To help him deliver the White Man's words? You're a Cheyenne, you shouldn't be helping them."

"It was for protection. If something like this happened, I could communicate with the bands of Indians. Clinton has helped me so much, I needed to help him too."

"What has happened with the tribe?"

"Mainly women, children and elders were spared and taken as prisoners — a few warriors as well. We are doing the best we can. It has been a sad time and our hearts are heavy."

"Why don't you escape and join us? This is your chance."

"As much as I would love to roam free, I cannot abandon the rest of the tribe. They need me. I'm the only one who can speak English."

"They should escape too."

"But how? There are guards that watch us. Lives would be risked if we attempted to escape."

"We could come up with a plan."

"Where would we go, Black Beaver? The army would catch up with us and every other band out there. They hire Indians to track us. I have seen the devastation they leave behind."

"Wouldn't it be better to have freedom, no matter what

happens? I have seen the devastation as well. It breaks my heart every time I think about it."

"Yes, freedom is everything, but I need to keep the women and children safe, and if we did try to escape there would be casualties."

"You are just like Black Kettle. He would say that. You have his spirit with you."

"Yes, I feel his presence every day. Oh, Black Beaver, I wish everything was different and we could be together."

"I wish that too but this is my path now, there is no other. I will fight for my freedom, and if I go to the other side, know that I have fought for my people."

"Black Beaver, it is so good to see that you are okay. After you left that day, I was worried all the time and never knew if you were alive or dead. You look good, though you're a bit skinny."

"We have been on the move constantly. Game is scarce and we haven't seen buffalo for a long time. The White Man kills the buffalo, not for the meat but for the skin. We have killed some of the hunters, they are a disgrace. You look skinny as well. I imagine they don't give you enough food."

"No, sometimes there is not enough to go around. Clinton helps me with extra supplies, but we have to be careful that no one catches him."

"Who is this Clinton? Who is he to you?"

"As I said before, he is a friend of the Cheyenne. Please don't hurt him. He is a good man." It wasn't the time or place to tell her brother how she really felt.

"If he is your friend I will not harm him."

"Thank you, my dear brother."

The rest of the dog soldiers were still mounted close behind Black Beaver and Morning Dove. Black Beaver turned around to explain the situation to Red Panther in his native tongue. Red Panther instructed him to obtain the White Man's words, they cannot be taken to the fort and if they are not handed over, his life is in danger.

"But we cannot let him deliver the White Man's words. You must hand the letter over."

"Very well, I will go back to Clinton."

Black Beaver and Morning Dove mounted their horses with the dog soldiers following. Black Beaver informed them, "He is a friend to my sister and the Cheyenne. There is no need to scalp him."

They nodded in agreement.

"Come on, sister, let me meet this White Man."

Clinton could hear galloping coming towards him. He was hidden under a cluster of trees after the bluff. He started to sweat and felt weak at the knees. *This could be the end*, he thought to himself. He dismounted Ranger and perched himself in a tree. There was nowhere to run, as the Indian horses were too swift for Ranger. It was better to make a stand. Clinton got his gun ready. He wasn't going down without a fight.

"Clinton. Clinton. Where are you? It's okay, they are not going to hurt you. It's alright." Clinton heard Morning Dove, but wasn't totally convinced. *What if it's a trap?* "Clinton, it's Morning Dove. It's safe to come out. I've told the dog soldiers all about you. My brother is here. It's safe. Clinton, where are you?"

"I am up here."

The dog soldiers saw Clinton perched in the tree and started laughing, talking in their native tongue.

"You need to come down. It's alright," Morning Dove said.

"Are you sure?"

"Yes."

Clinton made his way down, stumbled and landed on his behind. The dog soldiers burst out laughing.

"Are you alright?" Morning Dove asked, concerned.

"I'm fine." He got to his feet, feeling very embarrassed.

"Clinton, they want the dispatches that you are carrying. They do not want you to deliver the White Man's words. You must surrender it, it is part of the deal for them not harming you."

"I don't want to hand them over. No, I cannot. It would be treason."

"You must. If you don't I'm not sure what they will do."

Clinton thought about it for a moment. If he didn't hand them over, the Indians would likely kill him and take the dispatches anyway, but if he gave them what they wanted they would let him go. He could report that he was attacked by Indians who stole the dispatches. The general would believe that and hopefully not have him up on charges.

"Okay, I'll give them to you." Clinton reached into one of the saddle bags hanging from Ranger and handed the dispatches to Black Beaver.

"Clinton, this is my brother, Black Beaver."

Clinton extended his hand, but Black Beaver refused to shake it.

Clinton was impressed by Black Beaver's physical appearance and knew if he ever met him in battle, he would lose. He looked strong and must have conquered many enemies in his time. The other dog soldiers were equally impressive. Clinton had never been so close to warriors before. He stared at them in awe.

"I hope you are looking after my sister, soldier boy."

"Yes, of course."

"As long as you do that then I am you friend, but if you harm her, you will be missing a scalp."

Clinton was silent.

"Black Beaver, Clinton has been wonderful. Give him a chance."

"Well, Morning Dove, he must be the exception as most Whites I've met want us dead so they can take our land and women."

"Clinton has been an absolute gentleman. He is my protection."

"Alright, you don't have to convince me anymore. Morning Dove, there is much to catch up on. Our camp is not too far from here."

Morning Dove hesitated for a moment. "It's better if we don't know where your camp is. Just in case someone sees us with you. They will force the information out of us."

"Very well, let's sit here."

Clinton moved away to give them space. He led Ranger with him, who was acting uneasy, nervous about the enemy being so close. The dog soldiers all dismounted, letting their horses pick some grass, and went in the opposite direction to Clinton.

"My heart is so happy to see you, dear sister."

"Mine too, dear brother. There is so much that has happened. I have told you I am at Camp Supply at the moment, but I think they are going to move us to a reservation. When and where I do not know."

"Does your friend know?" Black Beaver asked.

"He does not know what will happen, but I have been feeling really uneasy about things. I want to be here in my home where my heart is, where the wind blows, the birds sing and the animals frolic."

"Don't go back. Come with us."

"What life would that be? Moving about all the time, worried about soldiers invading our camp. I would slow you down. I have to go back. If I don't, Clinton will get in trouble and may be punished."

"That's the White Man's rules, not ours, and this is your chance to be free."

"But for how long? I'm scared of what is out there."

"I know. I move about with the dog soldiers a lot. You cannot relax for a moment. It is an endless circle. We are free for the time being and that's important."

"But, Black Beaver, how free are you if you are always looking over your shoulder and wondering when you will be caught?"

"At least I can walk this earth without being confined, and dream under the stars."

"But what are you going to do now? What's your plan? You might be killed, Black Beaver. The soldiers will find you eventually. You should surrender, you will be safe. I don't want to lose you too. I'll have no family left. Please, Black Beaver, consider it. We can be a family again."

"If I surrender what am I surrendering to? A fat piece of bacon, some coffee and sugar. I know how the White Man plays games, making big promises and then taking them. They are tricksters like the coyote, but I have more respect for the coyote. Morning Dove, I think our destiny is going to take us on different paths. It is what it is. How I feel about surrendering doesn't sit well in my heart, but one day I may have to surrender. It is no life watching over your shoulder all the time, as you said before, but I think this is it for the present. I go on my path, you on yours. I will always remember and think of you. You will be close to my heart. So, how do you feel about this White Man?"

"Well, I like him a lot. He is wonderful," she said, knowing she still couldn't reveal her inner most thoughts.

"Morning Dove, please don't let your feelings go beyond that. It could become trouble."

"Clinton is so different from anyone else. Not all Whites dislike us. Look at George Bent. He helped Black Kettle a lot."

"I don't want you to get hurt. I'm not going to be there to protect you."

"I don't need any protecting from Clinton."

"Just be careful. I hate to part from you but we need to keep moving. I want to give you something." Black Beaver removed the elk leather spirit bag around his neck, which contained trinkets to ward off bad spirits, and pulled out a polished stone. Take this and whenever you are lonely, hold this stone to your heart and I will be there."

"I have nothing on me to give to you."

"What you have given me is all in my heart — the memories and your smile. Your smile will last me a million years."

"Oh, Black Beaver, I don't want to say goodbye. I may never see you again."

"We will meet again, whether it be in this lifetime or in the spirit world. Remember when we were young and Medicine Woman Later used to say how much you were like Black Kettle, even though he wasn't our flesh and blood. You remind me so much of him. It makes my heart happy that he was my father figure, a great man, a great chief. I think about him often. I know that he wouldn't agree with what I am doing. He was all about peace, like you. I remember on the night of one of our feasts, Red Panther accused him of being weak and demanded he fight the White Man, but Black Kettle was so steadfast in his belief of peace. I know he would tell me to surrender but my body is telling me to fight. Red Panther is our leader and if I quit now, he would tell me my heart is as weak as the White Man's."

"But, Black Beaver, it doesn't matter what people say or think. You should listen to your heart. I am not going to force you to surrender. I respect your decision. Speaking of Black Kettle, he always told me to respect a person's decision as you don't know why they made their choice. You would only know if you walked in their moccasins. Do not judge, just respect. He would respect your decision, even if he didn't agree."

The dog soldiers were leading their horses towards Black Beaver. "Black Beaver, we need to head back to our camp now," said Red Panther.

Black Beaver nodded. "Well, sis, it is time to part ways. I love you. Remember, I will be with you when you need me."

"And I with you when you need me."

Black Beaver and Morning Dove rose to their feet and hugged, not wanting to let each other go. Tears were running down Morning Dove's cheeks.

Before Morning Dove could wipe away her tears, the dog soldiers were gone. Clinton saw how upset she was and went to her, holding her in his arms. Morning Dove felt safe when she was with Clinton. She could hear his heartbeat and hers beating in unison. She didn't want to go back to Camp Supply. Maybe Black Beaver was right about her escaping now while she could, or maybe it was wishful thinking. Clinton would probably be punished if she didn't return with him and she couldn't bear that thought. She had to keep reminding herself that the White Man's world was completely different. She had to go back to Camp Supply but she knew eventually she would be taken to a reservation. This made her uncomfortable because she didn't know if she'd see Clinton again.

Clinton placed his hands on Morning Dove's cheeks

and wiped her tears. "I'm sorry, Morning Dove, that you have lost your brother again. You never know, eventually the dog soldiers may have to surrender and you will be together again."

It gave Morning Dove a glimmer of hope that she would see her brother again and she smiled slightly.

Clinton looked into Morning Dove's eyes, mesmerised. It was the right time to kiss her. He bent over and placed his soft lips on hers. A single soft kiss beckoned them and both pulled back, still looking into each other's eyes. The kiss tantalised their emotions and they both knew they wanted to be in each other's arms. Clinton stroked her beautiful silken hair. He placed his hands on her rosy cheeks and brought her lips to his once more.

Passion engulfed them. Clinton became aroused and never wanted to stop kissing Morning Dove. Their arms were interlocked, kissing passionately at first then slowing it down with soft sensual kisses. Clinton turned Morning Dove towards a tree, her back arching against it.

Morning Dove pulled back from Clinton. "What if someone comes along, like more dog soldiers? There are plenty of rogue bands around. We need to keep moving."

"You're right. We don't want to be surprised by Indians again. They would scalp me if they saw me with you," Clinton said. "Well, we better head back and tell General Custer that dog soldiers took the dispatches. Whatever you say, do not tell them about your brother — be very vague."

"What does vague mean? What should I say?" asked Morning Dove anxiously.

"Just say that dog soldiers ambushed us and found the dispatches when they checked the saddle bags, and that you didn't know who they were. You spoke to them in Cheyenne and told them you were Black Kettle's daughter. You convinced them not to scalp me. That's all you need to say, nothing more, but they might not even ask you. If you told General Custer that you saw your brother and he was riding with the dog soldiers, they would hunt them down and use you to help them. Let me do the talking."

Morning Dove nodded and both mounted their horses, starting the journey back to Camp Supply. There was silence for ten minutes until Clinton wanted to mention something.

"I have decided to take some leave to see my sister. I haven't taken leave since I joined the army, so I am hoping General Custer approves it. I need to take myself away from this environment to make a clear decision about us and what our options are, but don't ever doubt our love. We will fight to keep it. Are you okay with that? I won't go if you don't want me to. We can't sneak around forever. All I know is that I love you and want to spend my life by your side."

"Yes, you go. I look forward to the day when we can truly be together. But why does everything have to be complicated?"

"I don't know, but our love is worth it."

"I know, but I hate sneaking around. We cannot announce our love to people and we can never embrace in public," said Morning Dove.

"I wish we could gallop into the wilderness never to be found again," a hopeful Clinton stated.

"You know what would happen if we didn't return."

"Yes, but when you think about it, we could have been captured or killed by Indians. That's what they would think if we didn't return, not that I had deserted."

Morning Dove and Clinton looked at each other, thinking about whether they should take that chance.

"It is too risky," Morning Dove finally said. "I don't want to endanger your life. They would shoot you as a deserter."

"They would, but not if they didn't find me."

"It reminds me of Black Beaver's situation. He is always looking over his shoulder now and you would have to do the same, and one day they might find you and your life would be over."

"You are so wise, Morning Dove. You think about everything. Well, I guess we have no choice but to return."

21

Clinton and Charlotte's Reunion

Weeks had passed and Clinton was ready for his long journey back to Michigan to see his beloved sister. He was unsure what to expect, as the years had flown by without seeing her. He always thought of her and wondered about her new husband and if they were making ends meet. But for now, he needed to see Morning Dove. He'd overheard something that he needed to tell her. He found her walking around the camp's perimeter. She smiled when she spotted him. He nudged his head for her to follow him behind her tent, where they crouched down so no one could see them.

"I am about ready to depart on my journey. I am heading to Fort Hays and leaving Ranger there before catching the stagecoach and train to Michigan," Clinton said, keeping his voice low. "I heard that all captured Indians will be relocated to Fort Hays temporarily. It will happen soon — I suppose while I am away. Don't worry, I know where to find you. I have to come back to get Ranger. They are trying to work out a proper reservation as we speak. Don't tell anyone what I told you. I have got a long journey ahead of me. In about four weeks, I'll be back. You'll be okay?"

"I'll try to be. It won't be the same and I will miss you."

"I will miss you too and will think of you always on my journey. You will keep my heart warm. I better go now." Clinton departed abruptly before anyone could see him with Morning Dove.

Morning Dove stared at Clinton as he went back to the picket line to bridle and saddle Ranger. He led Ranger out of camp and winked at Morning Dove. They stared at each other for a moment, their eyes saying it all.

Morning Dove occupied herself as best she could without Clinton around to distract her. Her heart was heavy with concern that Clinton might change his mind about their relationship. *What if he doesn't come back? What if spending time away from the prairie makes him see things differently?* She felt unsettled.

Even though they were both from different worlds, she felt at peace with Clinton and never wanted to leave his side. She was fascinated by him. Her future seemed destined to be on a reservation when the time came, and her heart sank whenever she thought about it. She wanted to be free to travel anywhere without the army watching her every move. She needed answers, which meant seeing her grandmother.

Morning Dove entered her tent and found Runs With Horses alone. She was sitting in the middle of her tent, chanting to the Great Spirit. She stopped when Morning

Dove sat in front of her. "Morning Dove, your heart is heavy again. Didn't the Great Spirit give you advice?"

"Oh, Grandmother, I am so confused."

"Speak to me about your troubles."

"My heart is heavy because I am in love with someone who is not Cheyenne. The whole situation is complicated."

"I have known you for many years, Morning Dove. You have blossomed in front of my eyes. You always had your own spirit that travelled on a different path to most Cheyenne women, and I worried that you would never be a wife or mother. The Great Spirit made you who you are. You always did have a special light. Black Kettle loved you as if you were his own and always refused offers of marriage for you. He knew that you weren't in love with any of the suitors. And now you have found love with the enemy — an army captain is quite an unusual choice."

"How did you know, Grandmother?"

"I see the way you look at him. The eyes are the window to your spirit."

"Oh, Grandmother, what do I do?"

"My beloved Morning Dove, your path is what it is. All paths are different. You must follow your heart and the Great Spirit."

"Oh, but it seems too hard to be together."

"It doesn't have to be. You have created the impossible."

"What do you mean, Grandmother?"

"You have made people's expectations dominate your feelings and allowed it to suffocate your love."

"So, you are saying we are more worried about people's thoughts than how we feel about each other?"

"Yes. Love is pure and has no boundaries — it does not care if you are white or red."

"Oh, I feel so relieved now. Your words make sense, but what if people cause us grief?"

"Love can withstand anything, Morning Dove. It's only us who create barriers. Yes, you are in a complicated situation but change can occur and settle things. Our way of life is over. We cannot beat the White Man. My heart is sad that we cannot run through the wild prairie, but I have been fortunate to have spent most of my life free. For the young it will be a struggle to cross over to the White Man's world. Change is the only way to survive. Morning Dove, you will see that some traditions will fade over time. If you really do love this man, then that is your path to travel on. Our traditional way of life will never be the same. Maybe your destiny was to fall in love with this man so you can be a bridge to both worlds."

"I have been told that before in a dream. Sweet Medicine told me I was a bridge between two worlds."

"That is a very powerful message — it is your destiny. Don't be afraid to be different. Your heart will tell you everything — always listen to your heart."

"Thank you, Runs With Horses. I am so fortunate to have you as a grandmother. I feel so much better. I can't wait for Clinton to return."

"Morning Dove, you can live in both worlds, you know

the White Man's tongue and will have no problems adjusting, but please help your tribe. They need you."

"Of course, Grandmother. I will never desert my people. I am Cheyenne and my heart belongs to them."

"Make sure you tell your beloved. Don't let him take you away from your people. They will face troubled times and will need you to bridge the gap, that is your destiny."

"I cannot thank you enough for your wisdom. I know exactly what to do."

"Everything you need to know is here." Runs With Horses pointed to Morning Dove's heart. "The Great Spirit speaks to you through your heart. Follow its guidance. Don't ever be afraid."

Clinton finally arrived at Charlotte's cottage after a long journey. He knocked on the door, excited to see his sister. The door burst open, revealing Charlotte, Barbara and Grace, all with huge smiles on their faces.

Charlotte gave Clinton a long hug and didn't want to let him go. It had been a long time since she'd last seen him. "Good to see you, my dear brother. You look healthy — the outdoor life must suit you. I have missed you so much, so has Barbara and Grace."

Barbara and Grace gave Clinton a big hug and had to be encouraged to release him from their grip.

"I have missed everyone so much, especially you two." Clinton started tickling his nieces, making them giggle.

"Clinton, please come inside. I have a big surprise," Charlotte said.

Clinton followed his sister to the dining room, where he found Mathew wheeling a sturdy wooden style pram.

"Please meet my husband, Mathew and our two new additions, both boys," Charlotte said.

"Wow! Twins. I cannot believe it."

"I sent a letter to Fort Laramie about the twins. I hope you received it," Charlotte said.

"No, I didn't. I moved on from there. I must have just missed it."

Mathew shook hands with Clinton and introduced his six month old sons. "This is Clinton Junior and John. We thought it would be nice to honour yourself and your sister's late husband."

"Oh, my. I am flattered. It's hard to believe you have twins. They are adorable and have your features, Charlotte." Clinton picked up Clinton Junior and began rocking him. He placed him back down and picked up John, giving him a quick rock as well.

John began crying when Clinton put him back down, and Mathew took over nursing him.

"This is incredible. How are you coping?" asked Clinton.

"I am glad we haven't got triplets, or else I wouldn't know what to do. We are going all right, considering we have four children now."

"You two should catch up," Mathew said. "Off you go. I will look after the twins."

"Thank you, Mathew. Come on, Clint, it's a nice afternoon. Let's sit on the porch."

Clinton and Charlotte sat on the rocking chairs on the

porch, while the girls ran around with Mable, who was no longer a puppy.

"Twins is still a bit of a shock," said Clinton.

"I know, it was for us too — and the birth was a difficult one. Mathew was very worried about me, as I wasn't that well in the last three months. I was worried as well, not knowing what may happen. It is common for women to die during child birth — and I have heard some horror stories."

"I would have come back if you needed me."

"I wasn't sure where you would be. That is the problem with your job — trying to find you. I never know if my letters or telegrams will make it to you. I worry that you could be lying scalped in a field somewhere." Charlotte squeezed Clinton's hand. "I am glad you are here."

"Me too. So, what is this Mathew like? Is he good to my nieces and nephews?"

"Mathew is a good father. He has taken Barbara and Grace under his wing, but is fairly strict with them and rarely indulges in their games. He has bonded with the twins really well."

"Are you happy?"

"Mathew is a good provider. He works at his uncle's farm each morning, and his uncle pays him well. They are quite successful in providing the community with produce."

"That's not what I asked. Are you happy?"

"I don't know, Clint. I just don't know. What can I do? Am I happy with Mathew? He is not emotional and always has his guard up. There is not much passion, not like a husband and wife should have. I suppose I compare him to John and our marriage, which was blessed by god. This marriage doesn't even come close. I am hanging in there for the sake of the children. I have to see this marriage through. I couldn't manage four children on my own. When I met Mathew for the first time I was attracted to him. We courted for a short while. I didn't want to be alone forever. I had two children to look after and needed a husband. I'm alright, Clint. It is best to be where I am."

"But do you love him, Charlotte?"

"I thought I did, and I tried to convince myself that it was love, but I am not sure that I love him. I just can't see a way out. There is nothing I can do. Let's not talk about me anymore. What about you? How is army life?"

"The pay is shocking, the food is even worse, the Indians are hard to catch. It's dangerous but I'm fine."

"You seem different. Something has changed you. You have a glint in your eye that I haven't seen since you were a boy and in love with our neighbour Annie."

"Oh yes, Annie. I was in love, but she played hard to get. It just wasn't meant to be. I was heartbroken for months."

"Are you in love with someone, Clinton?"

"I can't really say — it's complicated."

"Why is that? She's not married, is she?"

"No, not married."

"What is it, Clint? Are you in love or not? Tell me, I want to know. If you can't tell your sister, who can you tell?"

"I am in love, but not with a white woman. She is a Cheyenne named Morning Dove."

"That's a funny one, Clinton. Ha! Ha! Don't scare me like that, and what kind of name is Morning Dove? Good one, Clint." Clinton didn't laugh. "You're not serious, are you, Clint?"

"Yes, this is serious. It is no joke."

"I think you have been out on the prairie too long. The sun has affected you. You can't be in love with this woman. Indians are savages — they come from a different world. What were you thinking? You are in the army and a captain. If anyone finds out they may revoke your position. Oh, Clint, how could you fall in love? You need to find a nice white woman and settle down and have some children. You need to forget about this Morning Dove. Leave the army if you have to. Have you fallen in love because you lost Nancy? You did write to me about her and what happened. Are you trying to replace her memory?"

"No, I'm not trying to replace her. What happened to Nancy I will never know — she just vanished. But I feel things for Morning Dove that I never felt for Nancy. It hasn't been easy for me. I wrestle with my feelings every day. My love for her is forbidden. I have never felt this way about anyone else. Everyone has so many assumptions about the Indians — that they are blood thirsty savages who are nothing but murderers and thieves, and the general public believe them. Yes, I have fought Indians and thought of them that way, just as everyone else does. That is what's wrong with society, people go by other people's opinions, by gossip and hearsay. No one has actually got to know them, to learn why they are angry with us Whites and go on raids.

"Being in the army, I have seen the injustices served to these people. Yes, Morning Dove has been a big influence on me and I have got to know the Cheyenne tribe. I see them as people now, not savages. They fought for their land, the land the White Man was stealing — the army and government broke so many treaties. The Indians fought and killed because they had to, but I am not saying there aren't bad Indians out there. All I am saying is we haven't given them a chance. We kill them without speaking to them first. Sometimes I feel ashamed to wear this uniform, knowing that it is a symbol of fighting Indians on the frontier. If you could just see them, the way they interact with each other harmoniously. They look after each other."

"Clinton, you have really fallen under this Morning Dove's spell. I have never seen you so passionate before. As a captain of the army, you protect the frontier. That is your job, but it sounds as though your job is affecting you."

"You are right, it is affecting me. I can't think straight. That's why I have taken leave to sort things out."

"Where is Morning Dove now?" Charlotte asked.

"She is at Camp Supply and was happy for me to take leave to sort things out."

"Oh, Clint, I can't tell you what to do. I am not the one risking my life for the good of America."

"Well, if I don't stay in the army I may never see Morning Dove again. I could never access the reservation that she will eventually live on."

"Just stay here for a while. We would love to have you.

Just stay until you know what to do. Sometimes when we are focused on something too much, the answers don't come. Try and keep your mind busy and eventually you'll know what to do."

"So you're saying I am going to be busy playing uncle to four children."

"Well, yes, you could say that." They both burst out laughing. "But, Clinton, it is so good to see you as I have missed you so much. I wish you would move back here and acquire a normal job so I don't have to worry about you getting scalped. I get lonely."

"How can you be lonely when you have your husband and four children to take care of?"

"I am lonely for adult company — someone who understands me. I am not sure that Mathew does."

"Perhaps you should meet with some of the women in the community."

"That may be a good idea but it is hard to find the time with four children. How are you feeling now?" asked Charlotte.

"I am more confused than ever. I don't know which way to turn. It is not me questioning my love for her. It's just a matter of getting around the situation we are in."

"Oh, Clinton, I wish I could help you, and I wish I knew Morning Dove so I could understand why you love her." Charlotte paused. "Being a captain makes this situation more difficult. I don't feel it would be proper for you to pursue this woman. She is an Indian and belongs with her own people. You cannot put her through all this. She has different traditions to us. It might be hard to conform to our way of life. You may love her, Clinton, but is that enough? Someone will have to make a big sacrifice and adjust to the other's lifestyle. You cannot live in two worlds.

"I am sorry, Clinton, but I do not feel it will work. You need to leave Morning Dove where she is. She belongs with her people. You need to find someone else, settle down and have children. I'm sorry." Clinton was silent. "Please say something."

"I feel as though my heart has been crushed. Our situation is hard on both of us. We never expected to fall in love — you can't predict these things. I honestly don't know what I should do. Yes, we are in difficult positions, but, sis, I need your support. I love Morning Dove and that will never change. I could never feel as I do about her with another woman — there is no one like her. But our love is forbidden and I cannot announce it to the world. Special people like Morning Dove don't come into your life very often. I love her not because it is right or wrong, I just love her."

"I understand what you are saying, Clinton, but you need to think about your future. People will never let you forget that you're with a Cheyenne. Can you imagine if you did bring her back here? What people would say?"

"Charlotte, I don't want to speak about this anymore. I wish you could see things from my point of view. I am going for a walk," Clinton said, disgruntled. He stood up and wandered to the vegetable garden, trying to find some peace.

A couple of minutes later, Charlotte appeared. "Clinton, I am sorry. I didn't mean to upset you."

"It is alright. What you said made a lot of sense. I just didn't want to hear it. I want a solution to all of this."

"I know, Clinton, and I really do hope you find one."

"Maybe it's not meant to be." Clinton sighed. "And you're right, I cannot take Morning Dove away from her people, that wouldn't be fair. If we were to be together, I couldn't have a career in the army anymore. What would I do? Maybe love just isn't enough. This whole thing is driving me crazy."

"Oh, Clinton, I have never seen you like this before. My reaction was not of a supportive sister. I'm sorry. I was shocked and I am sure other people's reactions would be much worse. Can you live with people's prejudices? I'm sure that I would like Morning Dove and if you love her like you say you do, I will welcome her with open arms. And remember if you do have children, they would be trapped in two worlds and people wouldn't let them forget it."

"It sounds as though you're trying to convince me to let go of this whole thing and not fight for our love."

"I don't mean to. I just want you to be aware of all the possibilities that could happen. I love you, Clinton, so much. I want the best for you, that's all. I hope you find a solution, I really do. I will support you with whatever you decide. I would prefer you to settle here and quit the army. I have been worried sick about you. You're a good man and deserve the best the world can offer, and if that means being with Morning Dove then I will go with that. Oh, Clinton, come here I need to hug you."

They both embraced. Charlotte had tears streaming

down her face. She had her beloved brother back, but for how long?

"Clinton, let's make the best of what time we have and enjoy each other's company. Let's put the wild west at the back of our minds."

"Sounds good to me. My head needs a break from thinking too much."

22

Clinton's Journey Back to Morning Dove

Weeks passed and it was finally time for Clinton to return to duty. He couldn't wait to see Morning Dove, though he still wasn't sure about their relationship and how it would work. He knew he loved her with all his heart, and her happiness and future were his priority.

Clinton, Charlotte, Barbara, Grace and Mathew were standing outside the cottage — the twins were sleeping inside.

"Goodbye, Charlotte. I will miss you so much. I will write to you when I get settled and let you know what is happening."

"Good Luck, Clinton. Be safe. Come back soon," Charlotte said with tears in her eyes, giving him a long hug.

"Mathew, look after my family for me. They are very precious."

"I will, Clinton. Have a safe journey." Clinton and Mathew shook hands.

"As for you two, my little nieces, be good and look after your mother while I'm away." He tickled them.

"Don't go, Uncle Clint," they said in unison.

"Duty calls. I'll come back, I promise."

"Here is some bread and ginger cookies for your trip." Charlotte handed him a care package.

"Thanks, sis. What would I do without you?"

Everyone finished saying their goodbyes and Clinton began his long and dangerous trip back to Fort Hays to reunite with Ranger and Morning Dove. The information he received before he left implied the Cheyenne would be there, or in close proximity. Along the way, he stopped at Fort Laramie where he spent two days catching up with his old comrades, especially Jacob, and visited Cimarron and Flash. The fort began to bring back unhappy memories, so he was glad when it was time to leave.

The next part of his journey involved catching a stagecoach — his most hated mode of transport. He always felt vulnerable to Indians and outlaws, as you never knew what was out there. He had a lot of admiration for the drivers — they had so much courage.

Clinton boarded the stagecoach and was surprised by the mixture of passengers, who struck him more as city folk who would be more familiar with the streets of New York than people you would find travelling among the prairie lands. *What are these people doing out here?* Fort Laramie was a thoroughfare for immigrants, but it still made no sense to him why these people were travelling to Fort Hays — or perhaps they were stopping at Fort Sedgwick. *It really isn't any of my business*, he thought to himself.

Clinton squished himself into the back of the carriage

and the other passengers introduced themselves. A pretty young married woman, Hillary, kept staring at him while she snuggled beside her husband, Harry. Maybe she liked Clinton's uniform, but she was making him feel uncomfortable. Surely her poor husband noticed her staring.

An old lady, Mary, sat beside him, humming church hymns. She was with her daughter, Scarlett, who seemed very nervous as they crossed through the prairie, constantly looking out the window.

On the other side of the coach, next to the married couple, was a well-dressed man with a top hat and a curled moustache, Dereck. He kept taking small sips from the flask in his pocket. His face was becoming redder and redder and Clinton assumed the flask was full of whiskey.

Clinton closed his eyes and thought of Morning Dove; she would give him strength through this ordeal.

Fort Sedgwick was their drop off point to freshen up and change horses. There were no Indians in sight and when it was time to board again, Clinton was surprised to see the same people get back on the coach.

Clinton fell back into daydreaming about Morning Dove. He wasn't sure how long had passed when he suddenly heard gunfire. Clinton looked out the window and saw Indians charging towards the carriage on horseback. "Indians behind!" he yelled. "We need to find cover. It's no use running. They'll soon catch up."

Scarlett fainted at the word Indian. Hillary was still staring at Clinton and her husband, Harry, froze in terror.

Mary was saying her prayers and asking for forgiveness. Dereck drank all his whiskey and threw the flask on the ground.

Clinton hanged out the window, instructing the two drivers on what to do, since he had experience with this kind of thing. "I can see a river ahead. We should cross it and then find cover. We will have to fight it out. It is the only way. If we keep running they will gain on us. Go as fast as you can, then we will have time to prepare defence works."

The drivers, Sam and Lionel, nodded, grateful that Clinton was there with them. They were urging the horses to go as quick as they could. They made it over the river, which wasn't very deep. Clinton quickly ushered the passengers from the stagecoach and unhitched the four horses with the drivers' help. They overturned the stagecoach to use as breast works in the upcoming battle.

"All men, we need you to shoot your guns and come behind the stagecoach. All women, lie low in that long grass over there and have the horses close to you. You will need them to get away if we are killed fighting. Don't come out of your hiding place if we perish. Stay there until nightfall before riding out," Clinton instructed. Clinton could hear the galloping hooves and the war whoops of the approaching Indians. "Hold your fire, men, until I give the command. Wait...Wait... Fire now!"

The Indians, about twenty of them, tried to flush the men out, firing arrows and shooting guns. The men fired back and hit a couple of them. The stagecoach was the perfect barricade and after a while the Indians retreated, taking their fallen comrades with them.

The stagecoach was riddled with arrows, resembling a pin cushion. Clinton inspected it while Dereck and Harry went to get the women and the horses.

"Damn it, the axle is broken. Do you have any tools to fix it?" Clinton asked Sam and Lionel.

"Yes, we do, but it looks as though it will take a while to repair," Sam said.

"So you *can* fix it?"

"I don't know. It looks badly damaged, but we will certainly try. I don't like the idea of being sitting ducks for the Indians to find," said Sam.

"We will keep watch for Indians," Clinton said. "We cannot move out of the woods until nightfall as there could be more attacks now they know where we are." Clinton couldn't believe this was happening. He just wanted to get back to Morning Dove.

Sam and Lionel went to work on the axle and looked upset. "Clinton, come over here. It is too damaged. We cannot fix it. It won't take the weight of the stagecoach," said Lionel.

"Are you sure?"

Lionel nodded. "Yes. The whole stagecoach will fall to the ground if we try and use it, injuring the passengers, us and the horses."

Clinton walked over to the passengers, who were sitting on the grass, looking nervous, panic stricken and exhausted. "There is some bad news. The axle on the stagecoach cannot be repaired, so the only other option is to walk and travel by horseback. We have four horses but I don't think we should have any more than one person on each horse, otherwise they'll tire too quickly. The women can have a horse each and us men can share the other horse. We need to have regular stops. We can't stay here, the Indians may come back. We will leave at nightfall. Any questions?" Everyone stared at Clinton, too fearful to say anything. "We will have to ration our food and water. I don't know how long it will take to get to Fort Wallace, but if we stick together, we will make it through."

Morning Dove was getting more worried as the days went by. *Clinton should have been back by now.* So many thoughts were running through her mind: had he decided he no longer loved her? Was he coming back? Her heart was broken. *Where is he? What's happened?* She felt sick in her stomach and wanted to crawl under a rock.

During the late afternoon, while Morning Dove was assessing how many supplies the Cheyenne had, a lieutenant approached her. "Morning Dove, I am Lieutenant Charlie Little. I am a friend of Captain Clinton McKay's. He asked me to let you know if anything happened to him. I am sorry to say there has been some bad news. Indians attacked a stagecoach, which was found by another stagecoach passing through. They informed the cavalry. No one has been found — there are no bodies. We presume they were taken captive or their bodies were taken somewhere else and disposed of. We believe Clinton was on that stagecoach as he should have been back by now. I am sorry."

Morning Dove ran away, tears pouring down her face. She hid in her tent, knowing the other women she shared it with would be outside preparing ingredients for their next meal. She couldn't show that she was mourning — no one could know she loved Clinton.

Runs With Horses heard her commotion and came into the tent. "Morning Dove, what is wrong?"

"Clinton's dead." Morning Dove collapsed, grief taking hold of her.

Clinton and the others from the stagecoach trudged through the prairie, looking out for Indians and outlaws. It had been a week since the Indian attack. The food and water were getting low, and they were exhausted.

The women were at the front, riding the horses. Dereck was riding the other horse with Clinton and the others walking behind. "Are we nearly there?" asked Dereck, turning around to face Clinton. "I am dying for some whiskey."

"You might have to practice being sober for a while. I don't know when we will get there. It will do you good to get all that whiskey out of your system. You don't need it. You just think you do."

Lionel informed Clinton, "I can see something ahead. A group of some sort, over yonder, near the horizon."

Dereck yelled, "Indians are coming! Indians are coming!"

The women screamed and Dereck fell to the ground.

The horse didn't raise a fuss and stopped and ate some grass. "I am going to die! I am going to die! I don't want to be scalped alive. God save me, please. I beg for your forgiveness."

"Dereck, be quiet," Clinton hissed. "We don't know who it is yet, just get up and grab that horse." Dereck obeyed. Clinton could see everyone getting restless and told them to stay still. They were near a small cluster of mountains. Clinton looked with his field glasses at the horizon and spotted a group of horsemen. They were far away on top of a hill. He could see a guidon flapping in the wind. "It's the cavalry, don't be alarmed."

"Maybe we could wave them down once they get closer," said Harry.

"Are you sure it's them, Clinton?" Lionel asked.

"Yes, I saw the guidon flapping in the wind." Clinton looked through his field glasses again. "Oh no, it is Indians. They are dressed in cavalry jackets," he said, whispering to Sam and Lionel.

"What do we do, Clinton?" Sam kept his voice low.

"I'm not sure. I don't think they have seen us. If they had they would be coming straight this way. We will stay low for a while, and please don't tell the others. I don't think they would cope — they are quite flighty."

"Do you think we will make it, Clinton?" Sam asked, concerned.

"I don't know. Everyone is exhausted and we still have a bit more to travel until we reach Fort Wallace. We just have to keep going. Food and water have been scarce. I hate to think what will become of us if we don't make it in time. I have tried to plan the journey with everyone in mind, having regular rest breaks and looking after the horses. If we didn't have the horses to rely on then it would make it much harder. We are in no condition to fight Indians."

The next morning, Morning Dove awoke in her tent with her grandmother intently watching her. The other women assumed she was sick and spent less time there, not wanting to catch a dreaded disease. "What happened to me, Grandmother?" Morning Dove asked, sitting up.

"You were distraught with grief. Just rest. You have suffered the loss of your love."

"Oh, Grandmother, what will I do? I am in so much pain it is unbearable. I want Clinton back."

"Yes, I know, but nothing lasts forever on this earth. Everything goes in a full circle. We are born, we give to mother earth and we die. Death shouldn't be seen as a bad thing. It will happen to all of us — some sooner than others."

"Why did he have to die at the hands of Indians?"

"I don't know. He has been taken for a reason. The spirit world is all around us and I am sure Clinton is around you at this very moment. One day, my precious granddaughter, you will see him again, just not in this world."

Morning Dove laid down and cried again. She couldn't mourn in public. She couldn't tell a soul, only Runs With Horses knew about her forbidden love.

Two days later the same lieutenant, Charlie Little,

approached Morning Dove as she was walking around the camp's perimeter. "Excuse me, Morning Dove. General Custer wants to see you."

Morning Dove gave the lieutenant a blank stare. She felt horrible and didn't want to go anywhere near General Custer. She just wanted to mourn. But she knew she had to obey orders, so with all her strength she followed Lieutenant Little.

They approached General Custer's tent. The flap was up, revealing General Custer sitting at his desk, talking to his brother. Lieutenant Little waited until there was silence before walking in. "Excuse me, sir, Morning Dove is here."

General Custer spotted Morning Dove waiting outside the tent. "Morning Dove, come in. Oh, you don't look very well. Are you ill?" He encouraged her to sit on the stool in front of his desk. She did so as her feet felt wobbly.

"Yes, sir, I haven't been well."

"You can see our doctor if you wish."

"No, that is alright. I am feeling better," Morning Dove lied.

"Please tell your people we are moving from this camp to Fort Hays, for your temporary reservation, in three days. We leave at dawn. That is all."

Six more days passed before Clinton and the rest of the passengers reached Fort Wallace. They collapsed in utter exhaustion, dehydrated and covered with dirt. The horses looked just as bad. No one could speak, their throats too parched. They were taken to the fort's makeshift hospital, where a doctor attended to them.

"You are lucky to be alive," the doctor said as he took Clinton's pulse. "In another two days or so, most of you would have perished from dehydration. Everyone needs about fourteen days of rest and lots of fluids. The women are in worse condition and may need longer. Where were you headed?" Doctor Wells asked.

"Fort Hays," Clinton said. "And the sooner I get there the better."

"Steady on, young chap, your body needs to recover first. You don't want to go out too early and become a victim of those wild Indians."

"I suppose you are right." Clinton closed his eyes and drifted into a deep slumber, dreaming of his precious Morning Dove. Through his ordeal, Clinton had realised there was nothing more important than being with the one he loved, and if he had to leave the army he would.

Two weeks later, the passengers from the stagecoach were almost recovered. Clinton was walking around the room, stretching his legs, when Doctor Wells came in to do his checks.

"How do you feel, Clinton?" asked Doctor Wells.

"I'm eager to get out there again. I'm ready, Doc."

"Okay, Clinton, I pass you as fit to travel but do it gently. Take plenty of rest breaks. Take care of yourself."

"Thank you, Doc, for all your help. Much obliged." Clinton was relieved.

Once Doctor Wells completed his rounds, Clinton said his goodbyes to his new-found friends, who would be staying for a couple more days. They were all looking well, sitting up or wandering around the ward or outside.

Clinton approached Mary, who was sitting up, reading her bible while Scarlett brushed her hair. "Mary and Scarlett, take care of yourselves. I am free to go back to Fort Hays. You're a tough little thing, Mary. God must be watching over you. All the best, Scarlett."

"Clinton, we wouldn't be here without you," Mary said. "I know you are unattached and so is Scarlett. I would love to have you as part of our family."

"I am going back to win my sweetheart, and I am sure Scarlett will find someone. Where are Sam and Lionel? I haven't seen them since yesterday."

"The army hired them to deliver goods back to Fort Laramie. It all happened very quickly. I am surprised they accepted the job. They had to move out at night so they didn't get to see you and say goodbye, but they did leave you this note." Mary reached into her pocket and handed it to Clinton.

Clinton read the note, which thanked him for saving their lives. "Well, that was nice of them. I hope they stay safe. Where are the others?"

"I think Hillary, Harry and Dereck went outside to get some fresh air," Scarlett said.

"Thanks, I'll go and find them. Good luck, ladies." Clinton stepped out of the ward and found the other passengers talking to a few lieutenants who had just finished their army drills. Clinton acknowledged the lieutenants and then spoke to Hillary, Harry and Dereck. "I have been passed fit to travel. I leave today." Clinton hugged Hilary and shook Harry's and Dereck's hand. "Take care of yourselves. Where are you heading next?"

"After our terrifying journey, we are heading back east and never venturing to the west again," Hillary said. "Dereck and the girls are coming with us. We are going back home. We leave in two days."

"That sounds like a good idea."

Dereck cleared his throat. "Look, Clinton, you were right, my drinking was a nasty habit. I have kicked my vice and feel so healthy, ready to take on the entire Sioux nation."

"Steady on, Dereck, don't set your sights too high. Just get back home safely. I better go now. I'm heading to Fort Hays."

"We will miss you, Clinton," said Hillary.

"Thank you, Clinton. Safe journey," said Harry.

Six weeks had gone by and the seventh cavalry had made a new residence at Fort Hays with the Cheyenne captives in tow, residing at a new camp called Big Creek. An Indian warrior named Storm Cloud was trying to court Morning Dove. The Cheyenne people were encouraging the courtship and pressuring them to marry, even though traditional courtships took years. The women wanted to speed up the process as Morning Dove was at marrying age.

A few weeks later the Cheyenne captives got their wish. Morning Dove was preparing for her wedding. She knew this was wrong for her but didn't want to disappoint her tribe, and she didn't believe in love anymore. Her heart was shattered and she didn't believe it would ever repair. It was easier to give in to her tribe than fight. She no longer had any energy.

Morning Dove and Runs With Horses were having a deep conversation in their wooden slat cabin. "Morning Dove, this is your special day. I know Clinton will be in your heart forever, but the tribe needs you to marry. You cannot be by yourself forever. This is the right time for you," explained Runs With Horses.

"Oh, Grandmother, if this is my special day why do I feel so bad? My heart belongs to Clinton and will forever. I don't know if I can go through with this wedding."

"Morning Dove, you must. Time is getting on and we need to marry you off as you have an important place in this tribe. Clinton is in the spirit world now. Memories and love will last a lifetime, no one can take those away from you, but you need to move on. Don't hold on to him." Runs With Horses smiled. "This is the right thing to do. You may not love Storm Cloud yet, but I am sure you will in time. It is a good day to marry. Happiness awaits you, my dear granddaughter."

Morning Dove nodded and changed into her ceremonial dress with turquoise beading before heading outside, where a woman was holding Prairie Moon. Runs With Horses helped Morning Dove onto the horse and the woman led Prairie Moon to a wooden shack where she instructed Morning Dove to dismount.

Cheyenne women raced out of the shack, eager with anticipation. They grabbed Morning Dove's ankles and arms and carried her over the threshold. Once inside, they pampered her, changing her dress to a special white beaded elk's tooth dress, brushing her hair and washing her face — all part of the Cheyenne tradition.

The wedding ceremony itself was quick and cheerful, filled with the beating of drums, singing and dancing. Morning Dove was relieved it was over, but was dreading the wedding night.

23

The Ghost

Five days later, Clinton breathed a sigh of relief as he entered Fort Hays, grateful to be alive and well. He made his way to the stables, smiling when he saw his horse. "Ranger, I'm back. I missed you, old friend." He scratched him behind the ears. "You wouldn't believe the journey I've been on. Oh, boy, it's so good to see you. You look well."

Ranger neighed and stomped his right foreleg in excitement.

Clinton heard footsteps and turned around, finding Lieutenant Charlie Little gaping at him.

"Captain McKay! Oh my... Oh my..."

"What's wrong? You look as though you've seen a ghost."

"I think I have. It really is you, isn't it?"

"I am Captain Clinton McKay. You do remember me, don't you?"

"Of course, Captain. It's just... We received a report that there was an Indian attack on a stagecoach and presumed you were on it and killed."

Clinton blinked. "Oh... well, I'm still alive." Clinton

turned to Ranger. "Did you think I was dead too, boy?" He rubbed the bridge of his nose.

"Your horse has been sold to a new lieutenant."

"What?! He is *my* horse. I will be talking to the general about that. I better let him know I'm alive."

General Custer and Tom had their backs turned to the officers' quarters entrance when Clinton approached. He walked in and pretended to cough. They turned around and gasped.

"I'm alive. I have had a very arduous journey, but I made it."

General Custer's and Tom's jaws dropped. They were speechless for a minute before Tom broke the silence. "Clinton, is it really you? We thought you were killed, especially after the stagecoach had so many arrows in it. No one could survive that."

"I have been stuck at Fort Wallace for two weeks, and before that I was trudging through the prairie lands with the rest of the passengers."

Tom hugged Clinton. "You look wonderful for a dead man. I have my buddy back. I'm ecstatic. Don't ever do that again. I have shed many tears. This is truly a wonderful day."

"It is good to have you back, Captain," commented General Custer.

"General, Lieutenant Little informed me that Ranger is someone else's now."

"I'm sorry, Captain, we sold him to a lieutenant. There are plenty of other horses to choose from."

Clinton's heart sank. He didn't want another horse, just his old friend — they had shared so much. Clinton left and made his way to the stables again. "Lieutenant Little, do you know who owns Ranger?"

"Lieutenant Alfred Jones, sir."

"Can you tell him I want to buy Ranger back. I will double, even triple or quadruple, what he paid for him."

"Yes, Captain. I will find him now. I did tell Morning Dove about the attack on your stagecoach. You may want to visit her. Apparently, she got married."

"What?! That cannot be true. You must have her confused with one of the other Cheyenne women. It must be another false report. Where does the army get their information from? I can tell you right now Morning Dove wouldn't get married. I will find her once you talk to Jones about my horse." Clinton scoffed at the notion that Morning Dove had married. He knew she would never do that as she loved him.

He waited in the stables until the lieutenant returned. "Tell me you have good news about Ranger."

"Well, Captain. I have good news and not so good news. Jones is happy to sell you Ranger back, but at five times the amount he paid. He's a bit of a sly one."

"Tell Jones I will pay five times the amount, but remind him I am a captain and can send him to the front line to flush out Indians — his money will be no good to him then."

"That's a bit harsh, Captain. It's only a horse."

Ranger neighed in protest and kicked his hoofs on the stable wall.

"Off you go, Lieutenant." Clinton waited. "How did you go, Little?" he asked when the lieutenant returned.

"Jones is now only asking that you match the money he paid for Ranger."

"That is great news. Thank you, Lieutenant. I owe you one. There we go, Ranger, we will be partners in crime again." Ranger pricked his ears up. "Now my luck is changing. I am going to see Morning Dove at the Big Creek Camp. You can come with me."

Clinton saddled up Ranger, just like old times, and headed toward Big Tree Camp. Once they reached their destination, Clinton's eyes scanned the camp, trying to spot Morning Dove. From a distance, he noticed a woman who had hair like Morning Dove's. He moved closer and the woman turned around, meeting his gaze. She gasped and dropped to the ground.

Clinton cantered Ranger to Morning Dove and jumped from the saddle, kneeling beside her as she struggled to breathe. "Morning Dove, it's me, Clinton. I have made it back. The report about my death was false. Just breathe."

Morning Dove tried to say something, but words wouldn't come out. "C... C..." She took a breath and tried again. "I thought you were dead. My heart couldn't bear it — knowing that you weren't coming back. I have married. I am someone else's now."

Clinton stood up, tears running down his cheeks. He tried to compose himself but the tears kept coming. He was in shock. They were both in shock.

"Clinton, don't be mad. I didn't know you were still alive.

I had to marry for my tribe — they depend on me. I didn't want to marry but I was all alone, apart from my grandmother. Please understand why I did it."

"I cannot believe you have married and so quickly. I am heartbroken. I think it would have been better if I'd perished out there. You were on my mind every second of the day. You inspired me to survive so I could make it back to you. You have destroyed our love — our destiny. What will I do now?"

"I am so sorry. When I heard about your death I was in unbearable pain. The thought of not seeing you, never kissing you again, I was empty inside. The Cheyenne see death as another journey. We are not afraid of it. The Great Spirit goes in full circle. It is part of life. Do you know how many of my people I have seen die? It is too many to count, and I knew, like them, you were in a special place somewhere. I had to adapt to your loss, Clinton. But I will love you always."

Storm Cloud saw Morning Dove sitting on the ground and ran towards her, telling Clinton to leave in his native Indian tongue. He lifted Morning Dove from the ground and carried her away. Clinton was heartbroken and left with Ranger. He felt he could never love again, and after a few weeks passed, he decided to take a position in Texas to settle the Comanche Uprising.

In those few weeks, Clinton's judgement was clouded. He couldn't understand why Morning Dove had married. Why did she move on from him so quickly? He loved her and only wanted to be with her, and now she'd given her heart to someone else.

Eventually he concluded that Morning Dove still loved him, and had only married because of a false report that he was dead, and because her tribe had pressured her to. He couldn't be without Morning Dove though. He loved her so much and, if anything, the ordeal he'd been through had made him realise life was precious and you should be with the people you love.

Clinton had accepted the position to stem the Comanche uprising when he wasn't thinking straight. He had left with the cavalry and was heading to Texas. Two days into the journey, he realised he was making a big mistake and may not see Morning Dove again. The army could move the Cheyenne and he didn't know how long he would be in Texas, or if he would return alive.

During the second night of the journey, Clinton couldn't take it anymore. He needed to see Morning Dove and talk things out, then he could come back here — he'd have to have a good excuse for his desertion though, something he'd think of later.

Clinton saddled up Ranger and snuck past his sleeping comrades.

24

The Confession

After two days' journey, Clinton made it back to Big Tree Camp and found Morning Dove crouched on her knees, planting corn. He tied Ranger to a tree and snuck over to Morning Dove, who turned her head and gasped. "Clinton, what are you doing here?"

"I had to come back and see you. I had to make you mine again." Clinton helped Morning Dove to her feet. "I know you thought I was dead, and you panicked and married someone else. I know you do not love him."

"Clinton, everything has changed now. I am married to a good man. I couldn't possibly leave him. It is simpler me being with him. It makes sense. This is where I belong, with my people."

"I cannot believe you are saying this." Clinton's heart ached. "When I was in Michigan, I saw these enchanting wild roses. I just stared at them. They took my breath away. They were like no other. It made me happy and content. It was a reflection of you — wild, beautiful and original. You are my rose, Morning Dove. I love you. I will do anything to make you mine. I will leave the army and whisk you away from this reservation. Our destiny is to be together. Morning Dove, you are my Cheyenne rose, and I want to wake up to you each morning. I know you are someone else's now, which I can't stand the thought of, but do you really love him?"

Tears ran down Morning Dove's cheeks. "Clinton, you shouldn't have come back."

"I love you and we should be together. I should have made a stand when I discovered you were married, but my heart was shattered and I couldn't think straight. That is why I left. Tell me you love me."

"I really shouldn't say anything."

Clinton put his hands on Morning Dove's shoulders and looked straight into her eyes. "Please, tell me how you feel. No playing games, and no hiding your feelings from me. Be honest."

"Oh, Clinton, I love you with all my heart, when I thought you were dead I felt as though I couldn't go on, that my life would never be the same. I couldn't mourn in public. My heart was broken into too many pieces for it to be repaired. When you came back I couldn't believe it. It was a miracle. In haste, I married another man. I thought you were dead, and my tribe was pressuring me to marry. They didn't know about my love for you, only my Grandmother did, and I was at an age where I must marry, so I did. Do I really love Storm Cloud? No. I love you, Clinton. I've always loved you, from that time I first saw you at Fort Cobb — you have forever been on my mind since. What do we do now?" Morning Dove asked.

Clinton combed a hand through his hair. "I don't know. I must return to Texas. I just left to be with you. It was very spontaneous so I need to get back as soon as possible. See those bluffs over there." Clinton pointed in the distance. "Meet me there tonight and we will talk in private."

"I need to do something first."

"What?"

"I need to divorce my husband the traditional way, by putting his belongings outside our tepee — or, I suppose, shack. Oh, I feel terrible as he hasn't done anything wrong."

"Morning Dove, he needs to know. You need to be honest with him. We deserve to be together. I don't like other people getting hurt either. He will find someone else who really does love him." Clinton glanced about to make sure no one had spotted him. If one of the cavalry caught him he'd be in big trouble. "I need to keep a low profile until tonight. Be careful when you come to the bluffs, there are sentries all about. I will see you tonight, my love."

Morning Dove found Storm Cloud helping tribe members dig the earth to plant seedlings. She asked him to meet her at their shack where she waited for him on a rickety chair, fiddling with the hem of her dress. She gulped when he walked in. *You love Clinton*, she reminded herself. "Storm Cloud, there is something important I have to tell you, and it is not easy for me to say. I don't love you like I should. We need to separate."

"What do you mean you don't love me? Don't tell me

there is another man? It's not that blue coat I saw you talking to, is it?" He looked intently at Morning Dove. She didn't say a word, only turned away. "It is him. Why? How could you fall in love with a white man and a soldier too? Do you not see they want us all dead? They treat us like animals. This tribe will disown you. You are turning your back on your own people. Why would you do such a thing? You disgust me. I don't ever want to see you again. Good riddance." He stormed off.

She sprang up, tears staining her cheeks, and threw Storm Cloud's belongings from the cabin before running to her grandmother for safety. Runs With Horses was sitting outside a cabin with some other elders, sewing beads on moccasins. She spotted Morning Dove and stood up, ushering her to follow her to her cabin.

"Grandmother, Clinton has come back," Morning Dove said when she was away from prying eyes. "He confessed his love for me. I have divorced Storm Cloud. My future is with Clinton now. The Great Spirit was right all along." Runs With Horses listened in silence. "I love Clinton with all my heart. Oh, Grandmother, why did I have to get married? It complicated everything. I spent my wedding night with a man I didn't love."

"Morning Dove, you weren't to know Clinton was alive. That was the work of the Great Spirit. You married when your heart wasn't in it and I influenced you. I am sorry. I just didn't want you to be alone. It is hard to believe Clinton is alive. The Great Spirit works in very strange ways. Where is he now?"

"In hiding. He snuck away from his post without getting permission to leave. He has to get back as soon as possible. I am worried that someone has seen him. I am meeting with him tonight. Oh, my dear grandmother, you have helped me through troubled times. Your words are so soothing." She hugged Runs With Horses.

"Clinton must really love you if he risked his life to see you, and I can see that you love this man. It is in your eyes. Love always shows in the eyes," Runs With Horses said. "My time on Mother Earth is nearly at an end. I can feel it. I am many years old now, and when the ghost spirit calls, I will be ready. It is important that I know you are happy and with the man you love. I am worried about Black Beaver though. He is on the warpath. I fear he may be hurt or killed. I pray for him each day."

"I pray for Black Beaver too." She squeezed her grandmother's hand. "I need to meet Clinton tonight. I have to plan how to get to him. And then he will be heading back to Texas — it will be hard being separated from him again."

"Maybe you should go with him."

Morning Dove frowned. "But what about the tribe? I can't abandon my people — or you."

"We will be alright. You must follow your heart."

Morning Dove was standing outside her shack, staring at the night sky and praying to the Great Spirit for safe passage. She went to see Prairie Moon, her stomach twisting into knots, and hid her bridle under her buckskin jacket.

She had a satchel that Clinton had given her, which she flung over the horse's neck, along with a buffalo robe. She tied cloth over Prairie Moon's hoofs to silence her walking before leading her horse through the camp, stopping and looking attentively like an owl every few steps. Her heart was beating so fast she thought it might give out.

Mist swept across the horizon, slowly hovering into the camp's grounds. The sentries were at the camp's boundary, laughing at something. Their laughter echoed through the valley. Morning Dove saw Runs With Horses walk into the middle of camp. *What is she doing?*

Runs With Horses fell to the ground, pretending to faint. The sentries turned around when they heard a thud. They laughed again, thinking she was drunk and made their way over to her. Morning Dove knew it was a ruse and this was her only chance. She moved swiftly through the camp. Prairie Moon ran with her, the fog concealing their escape. They made it safely out, avoiding detection, but they still needed to make it to the bluffs. They ran towards a large shrub, hiding behind it so Morning Dove could catch her breath. She removed the cloth from Prairie Moon's hooves and leapt onto her back with such force she nearly landed on the other side. She galloped away into the darkness, ready to find her one true love.

Morning Dove approached the bluffs. "Clinton, are you there? Clinton? Clinton?" Morning Dove called softly.

The bushes rustled. "Morning Dove, over here."

Morning Dove urged Prairie Moon towards the bushes

and Clinton appeared with a welcoming smile. Morning Dove jumped off Prairie Moon and rushed to him, nearly bowling him over. They embraced and kissed passionately as if tonight was the final night of their lives.

Reluctantly, they broke away from each other and stared, not believing they were actually together, with no one around them — just the magic of the night.

"I have a busy journey ahead tomorrow. I'm going to leave very early in the morning, while it is still dark. I need to give Ranger a good rest before we commence our long journey. I would probably have left tonight but I am thinking of Ranger," Clinton said.

"Should I come with you to Texas?"

Clinton was silent. "Is that what you want? I didn't think you wanted to leave your tribe."

"I don't want to be separated from you again. And Grandmother said I should follow my heart."

Clinton was silent again, his mind going over all the scenarios if Morning Dove travelled with him. "As much as I want you to be with me, I don't think it is safe for you to come. Once I get to Fort Richardson there will be nowhere for you to stay, and there are Cheyenne enemies out there. As much as it pains me to say this, it is safer for you here. I know where to find you when I return."

Morning Dove started crying. Clinton hugged her and then sat on the ground with her under a confer tree, holding Morning Dove in his arms. "It will be alright. I don't want to be separated from you either, but I'm thinking about your safety. I love you, Morning Dove. Nothing will change that. I was a fool for taking an assignment in Texas. I thought it would be a good diversion for my broken heart."

"I love you, Clinton, and it will be unbearable to have you far away, never knowing if you're okay."

They sat there for a while, just holding each other, until they eventually drifted off to sleep.

The morning came quickly, with the meadowlarks singing their favourite tune. Clinton's eyes flew open and he gasped. He was meant to leave while it was still dark, but the sun had already begun rising. He quickly woke Morning Dove who began to panic as she was meant to use the cover of darkness as well to get back to camp. They jumped up, gathering their gear and organising the horses. They were about to mount when...

Six blue uniforms appeared. "Captain Clinton McKay, you are under arrest for deserting your post."

Before Clinton could do anything, one of the soldiers put shackles on his wrists. His fear-filled eyes were transfixed on Morning Dove who started crying. She didn't know if she should run or stay by Clinton's side.

"What are you doing here with a squaw?" The soldiers started laughing and sneering. "Well, I suppose we know. Night time can get lonely out here," said one lieutenant. They laughed again.

Clinton lunged at them, wanting to take them down. Rifle butts hit his mouth and blood spluttered out. Captain Worsley was approaching from the rear.

"What is going on here, Lieutenants? I asked you to

arrest the man, not harm him. He is one of us and the charges haven't been proven yet. Captain McKay, my apologies for your rough treatment. You are under arrest for deserting your post. An Indian scout brought back a message that you deserted in the middle of the night. I am sorry, Captain, but I must do my duty," said Captain Worsley in a sympathetic manner.

Clinton was still stunned at what was happening. He wiped the blood from his mouth and spoke. "Captain, what is going on? How did you find me?"

"You are a wanted man with the United States Army, Captain. An Indian named Storm Cloud reported through a translator that he had seen you here. We were searching around the area. We knew you wouldn't be too far. This is really serious. If you don't have a valid excuse, you are going to be in a real mess. So, Captain, why did you leave your post?"

Clinton looked at Morning Dove, their eyes staring at each other for what seemed an eternity.

"Captain, speak to me. Why did you do it?"

"I wanted to see Morning Dove. I was going straight back to my post this morning."

"But this squaw is meant to be on the reservation. What are you saying? That you love this Indian and she was going to escape with you?"

"Yes. I love her and I came back to tell her. Please, Captain, just let us go. We are not causing any trouble. I am going to report to my post."

"I am sorry, but I can't do that. You are under arrest. Take him to the guardhouse."

Six army personnel, who had earned respect within the cavalry, were put in charge of Clinton's fate. General Custer was excused from presiding over Clinton's trial, as he was personally linked to Clinton through his brother Tom.

The trial was being conducted in General Custer's office at Fort Hays. Clinton sat in front of the six presiding cavalrymen, with his hands cuffed and guards standing behind him. Clinton confessed his innocence and explained the truth. The cavalry all knew about Morning Dove now and didn't believe leaving his post to confess his love was a good enough excuse.

After much discussion, Clinton was found guilty of deserting and sentenced to death by firing squad in eight days. He was taken back to the guardhouse and put in a small cell. After the trial, Tom visited Clinton, finding him sitting with his head cupped in his hands. "Clinton, I am so sorry for what has happened. Running away in the night was a foolish thing to do. I managed to get my brother to telegraph a letter to the War Department about the possibility of getting you a pardon. I reminded him that he deserted his post to check on his wife during a cholera epidemic. My brother has many contacts and is very convincing. He will make a good case for you. Oh, Clinton, is there anything else I can do?"

"I don't know, Tom. I should have known that I would be caught. It was a risk, and I took that chance, but it didn't work out." Clinton sighed. "If there isn't a miracle soon and I don't make it, please look out for Morning Dove, and tell my sister what happened to me. I don't want to worry her, not if there's a chance I could get out of this."

"I will do whatever I can for you. I have spoken to Morning Dove and told her about the sentence. She is having a hard time about it."

"How did everything go so wrong? I can only hope your brother's telegraph works and I get a pardon. Thanks, Tom, for being here and trying to help me. I feel so hopeless and worried that my life may be over in eight days."

"Just hang in there and we will get you out. I'm not losing my best friend."

25

Saving Clinton

Morning Dove knew that she had to do something to help free Clinton, and there was only one person who could advise her how — her brother. On the day Clinton was sentenced, she escaped with Prairie Moon during the night. She told no one where she was going, not even her beloved grandmother. She rode for most of the night and then slept above a creek bed, amongst the trees for shelter. She let Prairie Moon pick at some grass while she closed her eyes to get some rest. Her thoughts were entirely of Clinton, knowing that in eight days he would be... She could not bear to think about it.

Morning Dove felt something nuzzle her face. Her eyes flew open and she breathed a sigh of relief when she saw Prairie Moon staring down at her. The sun had risen, which meant she need to get moving, but not before she prayed. "Oh, Great Spirit, please guide me safely to my brother. I don't want to lose my true love. He does not deserve to die. Please help me. Thank you for allowing me to escape to come on this journey and for your guidance so far."

Morning Dove hoisted herself onto Prairie Moon and ventured into the open prairie, not knowing which way to go. Suddenly, her heart felt less heavy with fear and her body became lighter. The Great Spirit was with her.

Her instincts told her to go right, further on to a group of trees in the distance. She trotted Prairie Moon to them and gazed around, deciding what direction to go next. Her eyes widened when she saw horsemen coming towards her. She panicked and steered Prairie Moon further into the trees. They were still a fair way off and she'd already been partially hidden by the tress so she didn't think they'd spotted her. She needed to find out who they were — friend or foe — so she climbed a tall, sturdy tree to get a better look.

Voices travelled to her on the wind and she recognised the Cheyenne tongue. "Dog Soldiers! Dog Soldiers!" she screamed in relief and hurried down. She was so excited she misplaced her step and crashed to the ground with a big thud. She ignored the pain and jumped up, using a fallen tree as a mount to get on Prairie Moon's back. She rode her out of the trees and waved at the dog soldiers, about ten of them, and they cantered towards her.

When they stopped in front of her, Morning Dove recognised no one. "I am Morning Dove, from Black Kettle's tribe. I have travelled from Fort Hays to find my brother, Black Beaver. He is with the dog soldiers, and Red Panther was the leader of his clan. Do you know where he is?"

"You have come a long way," said one of the Indians. "I am Red Raven. I know where Red Panther's tribe is camped, but you must give me your word you will not reveal its location to anyone."

"You have my word. Is my brother alright?"

"Yes. He is leader now—Red Panther died in a skirmish with miners," Red Raven said. "Life is hard now. We cross paths with the Whites often. They are always trespassing in our territory. We were surprised to see a Cheyenne woman alone in these parts. It is not safe to be by yourself. We will offer you safe passage to your brother."

The dog soldiers' camp was hidden in a rich, fertile valley. Red Raven led Morning Dove into it, where Black Beaver was attending to his horse. He turned around when he heard hoof beats approaching and his jaw dropped in disbelief.

Morning Dove leapt off her horse and ran to him, hugging her brother with tears in her eyes.

Black Beaver composed himself. "Morning Dove, I cannot believe you are here. How did you find me?"

"Oh, my dear brother, it is so good to see you. I didn't know what to do. I didn't know who else to turn to. I escaped from the reservation. Oh, Black Beaver, I am going to lose the man I love."

"What are you saying? Who is the man? Is it Clinton? Come, sit down." Black Beaver pointed to his buffalo skin mat, which was out in the open — they didn't have the luxury of tepees.

"How did you know?" asked Morning Dove once she was settled with her brother on the ground.

"Let's just say the spirits told me, but why are you going to lose him?"

"He deserted his post so he could declare his love for me. He was going to return to his post, but the army ambushed us before he could and arrested him. Before that Clinton was missing, presumed dead. I thought I would never see him again, but he came back. He is going to die, Black Beaver. I don't know what to do." Morning Dove sobbed on Black Beaver's arm.

Black Beaver stared at her in disbelief. "My dear sister, I love you, but when we enter a world that has different rules and regulations it can hurt us. I had a funny feeling about you both when I first saw Clinton. I knew there was more there than you let on, and that is why I warned you to become nothing more than friends. The whites have their own rules. What can I do? If I go anywhere near the fort I will put the dog soldiers' lives at risk. I am sorry, Morning Dove, I really am for Clinton. I don't want you to lose the man you love, even if he is a White."

"Black Beaver, please help me. I don't know what to do," pleaded Morning Dove, crying uncontrollably.

"You need to rest, you look exhausted. Stay at our camp for the time being. Let me think this through."

Morning Dove woke up the next morning on Black Beaver's buffalo skin mat. She felt disillusioned, not knowing where she was, then reality hit her and she felt sick. *Why is this nightmare happening?*

"Good morning, Morning Dove," Black Beaver said, walking over to her. "We are moving out."

"Where are we going?"

"Just trust me and pray to the Great Spirit. You will need to leave Prairie Moon here as she can't endure another hard journey. You can ride my black mare."

Morning Dove did as she was told, trusting her brother.

It took one and a half days of hard riding to get within the proximity of Fort Hays. The horses needed to rest, so they spent a day laying low and planning a secret attack. They located a ravine covered with heavy foliage that offered protection. There was also a small river that provided water for the horses and themselves. Black Beaver approached Morning Dove while she helped to water the horses.

"Morning Dove, you need to get back and find out any information you can about Clinton and what time his execution is going to take place," Black Beaver said. "Do it in the cover of darkness. I will send Red Crow with you."

Once darkness approached Morning Dove and Red Crow snuck towards the fort. Morning Dove led the way — after all, she was an expert at dodging the sentries. They made it into the fort grounds and towards the guardhouse. To their surprise, there was no one standing guard outside. They ran in, startling Clinton who was sitting and drinking coffee that someone must have snuck to him.

Clinton leapt up. "Morning Dove, is that you? Where have you been?"

"I needed to get help. This is Red Crow."

"Morning Dove, what are you up to? Please don't endanger your life by helping me."

"Black Beaver and the dog soldiers are here to help. We're still working out a plan."

"What?! Oh no, Morning Dove, please don't get the entire Cheyenne dog soldiers involved. I don't want anyone losing their life. I have accepted I may die. I don't regret coming back to confess my love for you. My love has no boundaries for you. It is ever flowing and will never stop. No matter what happens, always remember that."

"We will get you out somehow and then we can be together. Don't underestimate the dog soldiers."

"Tom Custer has just informed me that I won't be getting a pardon. He is still fighting for me, but it doesn't look good. I have four days of life left."

"Oh, Clinton, I feel this is all my fault."

"It's not. I made my choice, and I stand by it."

"Do you know when the..." Morning Dove swallowed, tears burning her throat. "When the execution is scheduled. The dog soldiers need to know the time."

"Twelve, noon. If the dog soldiers are my only hope, I give thanks to them and bless them." Clinton's gaze went to the door behind Morning Dove. "I think the guard is coming back shortly. You must go."

"I love you," Morning Dove said, and snuck away with Red Crow to hide in the stables. She managed to steal a scrawny piece of paper and blunt pencil from the guardhouse, which she used to scrawl a message to her brother.

She gave it to Red Crow who swiftly made his getaway to the dog soldiers.

Morning Dove woke early, having spent the night in the stables, and quietly made her way back to the guardhouse. No one was there, having gone to breakfast. She held Clinton's hands through the toughened steel cell bars. "Oh, Clinton, I love you so much. If anything happens to you, my life won't be worth living. I couldn't love anyone like I love you."

"None of that silly talk. Of course your life would be worth living. Promise me you won't do anything silly. You are an intelligent woman, and the Cheyenne need you. Live your life and don't be afraid to love again. I will always be with you." Tears ran down Clinton's cheeks.

Morning Dove nodded, her throat too thick with tears to speak. They stared at each other, not sure what was going to happen, hoping there would be a miracle. Morning Dove headed back to be with the dog soldiers and report everything about the fort.

The dreaded morning had arrived. Morning Dove was beside herself, terrified she was going to lose the man she loved, but she trusted her brother wouldn't let her down. A guard brought Clinton out. His hands weren't shackled, so they'd at least given him that dignity. Tom was beside him, weeping.

Morning Dove was in the middle of the fort with a handful of other Indians. They'd wrapped blankets around themselves to conceal their identities. The soldiers didn't take any notice of them, more concerned with waiting for the clock to strike twelve.

Morning Dove stared at the wagons full of hay, which were not far from her. *Come on*, she thought, and a second later fire arrows flew into the wagons, setting the hay alight. Fire arrows were also directed into the stables.

"Fire!" the people gathered cried and soldiers raced to put the flames out and free the horses, which sprinted through the grounds.

Whoops and yells filled the air and hundreds of dog soldiers swarmed the fort, firing and shooting. Every soldier jumped into action, leaving Clinton by himself. Morning Dove threw off the blanket and ran to him, pulling him towards the fort's entrance.

Black Beaver, who was mounted on his horse and holding two others just outside the fort, spotted them. Morning Dove raced to him with Clinton and each jumped on a horse.

"Get out of here as fast as you can," Black Beaver said. "Change horses at our camp. We will keep the soldiers busy so you have time to escape. I have the whole Cheyenne nation of dog soldiers here. It didn't take much convincing to bring them to fight the Whites. Go now."

Clinton was about to gallop off when a horse skidded to a stop beside him. His jaw dropped when he saw it was Ranger, who must have escaped from the stables. "It's good to see you, boy. Come on, follow us."

Morning Dove and Clinton made it to the dog soldiers' camp, where they rested for a little while, sitting on Black Beaver's buffalo rug. "Oh, Clinton, we are together at last. I cannot believe it. We have been through so much, but our love always remained steady and true. Where shall we go? I don't think I will see Black Beaver again. How grateful I am for everything he did. Did you see all the dog soldiers? What a sight!"

"It seems I will be a wanted man for the rest of my life so we cannot stay here. We need to go into neutral territory. I think I know just the place. I am sorry you may not see your brother again, and I will never see my sister again either, or my nieces and nephews — it's too risky. Oh, God, this is not what I planned." Clinton sighed. "There is no turning back now, we are stuck with each other, and to think, just this morning I thought I would never see you again. Life is unpredictable."

They knew they had to keep moving as they weren't out of the woods just yet. Clinton took the bridle and saddle from the horse he'd ridden and put them on Ranger, while Morning Dove prepared Prairie Moon. They mounted their horses and began their journey into the unknown.

Five days of solid riding, with little rest, passed by. Clinton and Morning Dove were in Montana territory, heading to the Canadian border. They stopped their horses and took in the amazing scenery — the mountains, the never ending sky, the greenery of the valley, and the endless rivers full of flowing water. They stood silent for a moment, breathing in the fresh mountain air.

"We are nearly at our destination," Clinton said. "See those woods over there? That is the border to Canada. Once we get over that, we'll be safe. Come on, let's go."

They rode their horses across the border, breathing a sigh of relief, before continuing on to find the nearest town. It took them a day.

"Look over there, Morning Dove, there seems to be buildings. Let's take a look." They rode towards the buildings, which they assumed were an indication of a frontier town. "Look at that, Morning Dove. The sign says, 'Welcome to Hope Springs'. It looks as if it is some type of mining town with a lot of people passing through. This is it. This is what we have been hoping for. What do you think?"

"If you think it is a good place, then go with your heart."

"Let's enjoy a decent meal before we do anything. I am starving."

"Do you think they will let me eat here? People act differently to Indians."

"I am sure it will be okay. You are not an Indian warrior, but a beautiful lady."

They found a small outside eating house and tied the horses to a hitching post. They wandered over and sat at wooden benches. No one said anything to Morning Dove about her not being allowed there. She was glad about that. They tucked in to plates of fried bread and venison stew.

Clinton patted his stomach once he was finished. "My

belly is full now, let's walk around town. I think these people are more open minded, but we will see." They began walking around, smiling at people in the streets. "Look, Morning Dove, there is a sign outside the general store, 'help wanted'. Let's go in. We will use fake names." They entered the store and saw a man behind the counter, counting money. Clinton assumed he was the owner and approached him, with Morning Dove at his side. "Hello, sir, my name is Henry Smith, and this is Sally. We are courting at the moment and have just moved to the area. As we were passing by we saw your help wanted sign. We are keen for some work."

"Pleasure to make your acquaintance, Henry. My name is John. I am the owner of the store with my wife, Mary. We are looking for help as we need to visit a sick relative and we will be gone for a little while. We need someone dependable, reliable and hard working."

Mary walked in from the back room. "I thought I heard voices."

"Come and meet Henry and Sally," John said. "They want to apply for the job."

Mary smiled. "Pleased to meet you both. We would like to have someone start as soon as possible."

"We will look after your store until you come back. You have my word," said Clinton, hopeful.

John rubbed his stubbled chin. "What do you think Mary?"

Mary smiled and nodded her head.

"Looks like you've got the job. Are you able to start

tomorrow morning so I can show you the ropes? There are quarters behind the store, which you are welcome to stay in, and there is a livery stable in town to keep your horses."

"Much obliged, John. We won't let you down."

Two days had passed, and Clinton and Morning Dove were learning how to run the store.

Clinton was stocking shelves with John and decided now was the time to talk about something that had been on his mind, as the store was empty and Mary had taken Morning Dove out to shop for garments. "John, can I let you in on a secret?"

"Of course."

"I am going to ask Sally to marry me. Is there a reverend about?"

"Oh, that's wonderful." John clapped his hands together. "There is a church on the outskirts of town where Reverend Timothy is."

"I would like yourself and Mary to be our guests and our witnesses."

"Of course, we will be there, but you might want to hurry up about it, as we are going to leave in a couple of days to visit Mary's sister."

Clinton tied Ranger to the hitching post outside the store and went to find Morning Dove in her quarters, having just returned from her outing with Mary. He whisked her away to Ranger, who they both mounted.

"I have a surprise for you," Clinton said.

"A surprise! I have never had a surprise before."

Clinton rode out of town to a beautiful creek bed with wildflowers growing and birds singing. Clinton dismounted Ranger and helped Morning Dove down, feeling nervous about what he was going to say. He clasped Morning Dove's hands and bent down on one knee. "Morning Dove, you are the love of my life. Our love has survived so much and we have become stronger as a couple because of it. I don't know what the future holds for us, but I know I want you to be my wife. Morning Dove, please marry me."

Morning Dove couldn't believe what he was saying. Without any hesitation she said, "Yes, I will marry you. Yes! Yes! Yes!"

The day had come to wed. Morning Dove was getting ready in her quarters with Mary helping her into a wedding dress. "What do you think of the gown you gave me?" asked Morning Dove.

"The cream colour and the slim fit suits you, and all the antique lace in the arms and neck makes it look classy. We need to do your hair and... Oh, I forgot we need shoes. Let me see what is in the store." Mary went into the store and returned with a pair of flat beige slippers. "This is the best we can do, and no one is really going to see the shoes, as the dress will cover them. Now the hair. You have such beautiful healthy hair. Shall we put it up or leave it down?"

"For something different, let's put it up. I always wear my hair out or in braids."

Mary found a large hair pin and pinned Morning Dove's hair in a soft loose bun, which she topped with white daisies. "I think we have done it, Sally. You are ready to marry. All we need to do is get you there. John and Henry are already at the church and John has hitched the wagon for us to arrive in."

"Thank you, Mary, for everything. You have been so supportive. You remind me of my grandmother."

"You're welcome, dear. Now let's get you married."

They left the store and climbed into the wagon, with Mary taking the reins and Morning Dove sitting beside her, feeling at peace. She thought of her brother and grandmother, hoping that one day she would see them again.

It didn't take them long to get to the church, where Clinton was waiting outside, smiling from ear to ear. He held his hand out for Morning Dove, helping her from the wagon. He was dressed in a navy dress suit that John had lent him. "You look beautiful. This is the best day of my life, finally making you mine."

Clinton led Morning Dove through the church to the reverend, with Mary and John following. Morning Dove placed her hands in Clinton's and they stared into each other's eyes while the reverend commenced the service. They said their own vows, with Clinton going first. "When I first met you, I couldn't get you out of my mind. You had found your way into my heart. We have been through so much through the prairie lands, but our love has always been there. I look forward to our new life together. I will look after you and treat you like my princess and forever be your protector. I will love you until the day I die."

Morning Dove smiled, tears in her eyes. "Yes, we have been through so much together, but the Great Spirit has finally allowed us to find our path together. We can grow old together and start a precious family, which I have always dreamed of. I couldn't think of anyone more perfect for me, so loving and understanding, but above all respectful. I, too, look forward to our next chapter, but a quieter one. I love you, Clinton — I mean Henry."

They were now husband and wife and were truly blessed to have found each other through all the turmoil. Hope Springs was the start of their new life together, what they were accustomed to would be no more. They had to pay a price for their love and that meant no more contact with familiar territory. They had to move forward together, but Morning Dove had the biggest sacrifice to make: she had to live in the White Man's world, with Clinton making all the decisions for her. Was she actually free?

Clinton, on the other hand, knew he couldn't go back to his beloved family. Would he be looking over his shoulder all his life? What if someone recognised him? Would he be satisfied with living in Hope Springs, or would the danger of army life beckon him once more?

Knowing Clinton and Morning Dove, they would work it out.

About the Author

Michelle's interest and passion for the American West started when she saw the movie *Dances with Wolves*. It prompted her to read as much as she could on this era and on Native American Indians.

This led her, in time, to travel to some amazing historical sites and national parks in North America, such as the Battle of the Little Bighorn memorial site, the sacred Black Hills in South Dakota, Monument Valley and Yellowstone.

She completed a historical fiction writing course that led her to develop the plot for *Whispers among the Prairie* and, with perseverance, to write a complete novel — her first.

Outside of writing, Michelle is currently studying veterinary nursing, and will be graduating this year. She loves all animals, but her favourite would have to be the Border Collie, so loyal, smart and a dedicated friend.

Lightning Source UK Ltd.
Milton Keynes UK
UKHW011414290321
381184UK00003B/902